'Thank you, Norah, for sharing the voices of women who remind us we can own and shape an equal and just future for all women and men everywhere. This book reminds us that work and care should not sit at opposite ends of one hard choice.'

— Elizabeth Broderick, Sex Discrimination Commissioner

'A book that makes you gasp in recognition and admiration, like asking for a promotion while on maternity leave, twice, and both times succeeding. Women's careers are interrupted, but as this book shows you can resume and flourish. Back yourself! Imagine a promotion or new job and plan to get it.'

— Hon. Mary Delahunty, Gold Walkley Award winning journalist, government minister, published author, non-executive director

'This book is profound and inspiring. Norah's masterful compilation of these exceptional women's lives points us to a recurring theme — that respect for women is everyone's business, and workplaces have the power to promote positive gender attitudes and make structural changes that encourage equal access to opportunities and resources.'

— Jerril Rechter, CEO, VicHealth

'How can organisations manage their workplaces in a healthy manner that recognises the reality that many people take career breaks? This book shares important insights that will be of interest to anyone building an inclusive workplace. It will also be a useful resource for people planning a career break.'

— Associate Justice Mary-Jane Ierodiaconou

Career Interrupted

How 14 Successful Women Navigate Career Breaks

Norah Breekveldt

with contributions by
Dr Hannah Piterman, Dr Jennifer Whelan & Samone McCurdy

M
MELBOURNE BOOKS

Published by Melbourne Books
Level 9, 100 Collins Street,
Melbourne, VIC 3000
Australia
www.melbournebooks.com.au
info@melbournebooks.com.au

National Library of Australia
Cataloguing-in-Publication entry
Author: Norah Breekveldt
Title: Career Interrupted : How 14 Successful Women Navigate Career Breaks
ISBN: 9781922129796 (paperback)
Subjects: Working mothers.
Women--Employment re-entry.
Career development.
Work and family.
Successful people.
Dewey Number: 650.10852

'How do you think it will be different, as a woman?'
'I have no idea, I've never done it as a man.'

— Anna Bligh, Premier of Queensland 2007–2012

Contents

Kate Jenkins

Kate Jenkins was appointed as the Victorian Equal Opportunity and Human Rights Commissioner in 2013. Kate brings 20 years' experience as a lawyer. Prior to this role Kate was the lead partner of Herbert Smith Freehills' Australian discrimination, equal opportunity and training practice.

Kate is the Vice President of the Board of Berry Street Victoria — the state's largest independent child and family welfare organisation. She is also a member of the Board of Heide Museum of Modern Art. Kate holds Honours Degrees in Law and Arts.

Preface

I was nine years of age when Victoria's Equal Opportunity Act was passed, prohibiting discrimination on the basis of sex and marital status. I remember clearly the newspaper reporting the plight of Deborah Wardley, a young woman who was consistently refused the opportunity to be admitted into Ansett's pilot training because she was a woman. Deborah was one of the first women to exercise her rights under the Equal Opportunity Act. I was 11 when the High Court of Australia determined that such discrimination was unlawful. In my young mind the time for such blatant discrimination was over, ensuring a bright future for women of my generation.

Jump forward to 2013. I was surprised to find I was often the only woman at the Board table, still consistently advising companies with male-dominated leadership teams. Many of my female peers had fallen off the career ladder or stalled after having children. Many of those same companies despaired at their lost female talent and the cost of the lack of diversity in their ranks. After more than 30 years of clear laws and good intentions, where were the women?

We have no doubt experienced progress since the days when women were by law paid 75 percent of a man's salary, and when they were required to resign employment upon marriage. But progress is not success. Gender equality has not been achieved, with women still earning less than men, retiring with half the savings of men, holding fewer leadership positions, and experiencing sexual harassment and violence at the hands of men.

It would be easy to be disheartened by this reality, but it is inspiring to see the huge groundswell of men and women now working towards accelerating the change towards a more equal society for the benefit of all. In 2013, I accepted the appointment as Victoria's Equal Opportunity and Human Rights Commissioner to add my efforts to the many people before me who have fought for equality. A closer look tells us that the slow progress towards equality in employment is now much more about slowly changing social norms than blatant discrimination. Few people now would share Reg Ansett's view that women were too emotional and unpredictable to be safely trusted with an aeroplane full of people.

We now know that good intentions are not enough to achieve change, nor are laws, though both are essential for progress. Change will happen when people are committed to equality for all. We know this happens best when people have empathy for others and when they can see a pathway to success.

I strongly believe it is the power of storytelling that provokes empathy. Stories can also show us that change is possible, and may in fact provide a better future for all. That is why stories, such as the ones in this book, are so important — and useful. They offer a range of perspectives from 14 amazing women, and I believe they are essential reading for men and women in order to inspire commitment to the changes we need.

The women featured in this book have some salutary messages for us all. They demonstrate that career breaks can result in exciting and unexpected opportunities that linear and unbroken careers often lack, and that brave choices can come from adversity. They also remind us that a career interrupted should not mean a career lost, and where it does, it is a terrible waste.

These stories illustrate the fact that flexible working does not equate to lesser quality or less valuable work. Each story reminds us that our families and personal lives influence every person's working life, and it can be a harmonious mix.

They remind us that others can stand in the way of our potential, deliberately or accidentally, but that others can be the very momentum behind our career trajectory. They reinforce how important it is to remember what influence we have on the journey of others when we are mapping our own pathways.

While they traverse a huge range of industries and sectors, I was delighted at how they provided insights into the common experience for all working men and women. Each story is a great read. There were some wonderfully frank admissions. There are marriages and divorces; successes and failures. There are lots of kids — not just one or two — and plenty of ideas about how that can work, even in busy working lives. There are great lessons about shared parental decision-making, support and misplaced guilt. There is also evidence of exclusion and injustice. Most of all, there are stories of resilience and wise decision-making, on the run and in response to opportunity, misfortune and the circumstances of life.

They will be well received, too, by the growing movement of men who recognise it is time to step up beside the women who have so long struggled for gender equality, to work together on this shared leadership issue. For men who have not experienced discrimination, these stories have the added benefit of revealing some of the invisible challenges faced by women colleagues. Norah provides an insightful framework for understanding the barriers caused by the social norms of gender stereotypes, the 'ideal worker' and flexible work as a women's issue. This thinking can help those leaders who look to change the structural and systemic barriers to gender equality.

These stories offer inspiration and give insight into how success was achieved by many women despite the ongoing barriers to equality. They provide plenty of ideas for anyone wishing to have a career break, for any reason.

I pay credit to every one of these women for sharing their stories, and to Norah for making sure the stories were told.

Norah Breekveldt

Norah Breekveldt is Director of Breekthrough Strategies, a leadership coaching and HR consulting firm. Norah supports business leaders to advance gender equity and diversity in their workplaces, and empowers women to create successful careers.

Norah commenced her career in the public sector, then progressed into senior executive roles in the chemical industry, motor industry, finance sector and supply chain organisations. As one of the few women on senior executive teams, she understands the dynamics of creating lasting change in complex, traditional organisations. She draws on this experience when providing insights to individuals, teams and organisations on embedding a culture of diversity and inclusion in workplaces and in managing individual careers.

She is the recipient of several awards, including the BCA/AFR Work and Family Award in 1993 for the introduction of work/families practices at Kemcor, and the Telstra Business Women's Award (Victoria) in 1995. In 1998 the Federal Government appointed Norah onto the Regulatory Review Committee of the Affirmative Action (Equal Opportunity for Women) Act.

Norah is the author of *Sideways To The Top: 10 Stories of Successful Women That Will Change Your Thinking About Careers Forever* (Melbourne Books, 2013). She contributes regularly to debates, discussions, professional publications, journals and blogs on diversity and inclusion perspectives, and is a regular speaker at corporate events and conferences.

Introduction

'A story is the shortest distance between a human being and the truth.'

— Anthony de Mello, *Walking on Water*

This book aims to contribute to the debate surrounding the lack of progress for women wishing to climb the career ladder in Australian workplaces, a debate that is becoming more strident in the public domain, and for good reason. Over the last few decades many women optimistically believed that with substantial legislative changes, greater female workforce participation and an established business case, permanent change would eventuate and the gender gap would disappear. Yet despite 30 years of social change, gender discrepancy in the workplace appears to continue unchecked, and the gap in earnings between men and women is as wide as ever.

Despite 60 percent of tertiary education graduates being women, in 2012 women accounted for only 9.2 percent of executive level roles in the Australian Stock Exchange (ASX) top 500 companies, only slightly up from 8.4 percent in 2002.[1] A scant 2.5 percent of CEOs in the ASX 500 were women and only 9.2 percent of Board directors were women[2] (although Board appointments increased to 19.8 percent in 2015).[3] Even where women occupy senior roles, men continue to dominate the mission-critical, hard-edged, financially driven positions behind significant business operations, while women continue to occupy stereotypical support roles in disciplines such as human resources, marketing or legal.

When it comes to pay, women are missing out at every level of their employment lifecycle. Even today, women graduates still earn around nine percent less than male graduates. As of May 2014, women's average earnings are 18.6 percent less than men's. In other words, women need to work an additional 66 days a year to earn a man's wage. The worst performing sector is currently finance and insurance, with a huge 29.6 percent pay gap.[4] What's more, women end up with only 59 percent of the superannuation of men at retirement, yet they live on average five years longer than men.[5]

Taking a career break remains one of the largest obstacles for women at work today. When women take time away from work they risk getting left behind compared to colleagues who stay and continue to make strides up the corporate ladder. Women also experience a wages penalty when they return, facing a fall in earnings of up to five percent after returning from a year's break, and over ten percent if they are away from work for three years.[6] Many women also feel that, as a result of taking time out from work, they take longer to get to senior level roles, and are often judged as less competent than those who have gotten there quicker. Although this is not just a women's issue, the burden disproportionately falls on women as they generally take more parental leave compared to men.

In the face of the undeniable research that women bring new knowledge, skills and perspectives to the table, and that diversity generates improved financial and share market performance, the status quo remains incredibly resilient.[7] We continue to recognise exceptional women and rare, positive stories rather than observe lasting and broad-based change.

From where did these stereotypes emerge?

Our sense of gender stereotypes, where women stay at home to care for the children and men are the main breadwinner, has been enshrined in the standard employment relationship in Australia since the 1907 Sunshine Harvester judgment. This judgment set a minimum wage for men based on an assumption that he would be supporting a dependent wife and two children, and have no caring responsibilities.

Women did participate in the workforce, but with the understanding that they would eventually fulfil their responsibilities as wife and mother — their 'real' job. So in 1950, the female basic wage was set at 75 percent of the male wage. Until 1966, married women were barred from permanent roles in the Australian Public Service. Wage equality between men and women was only established in 1974, although equal pay is still unrealised. Standard employment hours remain the norm in many workplaces, and returning to work after a break on a part-time job share role or flexible arrangement is adopted only in 'special circumstances' for a fixed period, or as a reward for good performance, rather than as an accepted way of working for everyone.

Research suggests that gender-specific programs and policies to support women in balancing work and family could consolidate the existing stereotype of women being the primary caregiver, while men can be free to get on with pursuing their careers.[8]

Prioritising and balancing work and family is difficult, challenging, time-consuming, and emotionally and physically draining. The burden of care continues to be shouldered by mothers regardless of whether they are working or not, thereby entrenching them further into a caregiving role and out of any real contention as a serious player in the workplace. But men miss out, too. Research by Samone McCurdy indicates that a growing number of men want to more fully participate in the care of their children. However, they continue to be frustrated by organisations who operate under the persistent paradigm of the ideal worker — a male breadwinner with a wife at home looking after the children — providing little or no opportunity for fathers to take substantial parental leave.

Where to now?

To achieve lasting and sustained change it's time to recognise that specific gender equality measures in the workplace is perhaps less relevant than promoting diverse workplaces and enabling parents to share parenting responsibilities. There is a growing body of research demonstrating that men who share the household chores with a partner have happier and less depressed partners, fewer conflicts at home and lower divorce rates. Caring for children can make men more patient, empathetic and flexible, lower their blood pressure, their risk of cardio vascular disease and their rate of substance abuse.[9] Fathers who spend more time with their children are also more satisfied with their jobs and are less likely to leave an organisation.[10]

Children of involved fathers also benefit. They are less likely to have behavioural problems, and more likely to succeed in school and their careers.[11] When dads and mums share housework equally, their daughters are less likely to limit their aspirations to stereotyped occupations. When children see their mothers pursuing careers and their fathers doing the housework they are more likely to practise gender equality when they become adults.[12] Finally, working mothers improve the future prospects of their daughters, who become better educated and earn more.[13]

The economy also prospers. Eliminating the gender pay gap could increase Australia's gross domestic product (GDP) by $93 billion, or 8.5 percent.[14] GDP could grow further to nine percent if companies introduced flexible work arrangements that make it possible for more women to re-enter the workplace. In the United States, 25 percent of GDP growth since 1970 is attributed to increasing women's participation in the paid workforce.[15]

If organisations are to reap the benefits of greater productivity and performance, and if the economy is to realise the benefits of growth, a new deal needs to be struck with working parents. That deal is about providing flexibility in working arrangements that make it possible for all parents to fulfil their family commitments as well as pursue a successful career. With the growth in digital technology, workplace flexibility is within reach, with many businesses evolving into virtual enterprises. It is becoming common practice to offer flexibility as a benefit to executives to encourage them back to the workforce after a break. However, the true workplace leaders take the concept further, providing flexible working arrangements as a standard way of doing business for everyone rather than an exception. A few leaders and role models include the Nous Group, multi-award winner of the BRW Best Places to Work awards, Justitia Lawyers, winner of the 2014 Ken Robinson Award for flexible work practices, Telstra Corporation's 'All Roles Flex' initiative, where flexibility is considered the starting point for all roles, health insurer Medibank as profiled in Dr Whelan's chapter, which has mainstreamed flexibility through Activity-Based Work (ABW), and Suncorp, where over 80 percent of staff work flexibly (including contact centre workers who work from home).

Final comment

Career Interrupted provides stories of high achieving women who talk openly about how they have navigated a career break. They describe the challenges of integrating their non-work lives with their careers. These women come from all walks of life — from battlers to more privileged backgrounds, from small business to big corporations, from professional services to the community sector. Several women talk frankly about what it's like to be in the throes of mother guilt and come out the other side, some are expatriates who returned to Australia to rebuild their career, yet others had to re-establish their career after a misstep.

Many of the stories at the heart of this book are about parental leave breaks, while others explore breaks arising from working overseas, ill health, domestic violence or having to resurrect a stalled career. Perhaps you'll find some of your own life stories reflected in these women's experiences.

Don't imagine an expert has written this book, or that it relates stories of women who have absolutely and flawlessly succeeded in managing the difficulties of a career break. There is no one right answer or right path; each woman has to choose her own path. Many of the women profiled in this book have done the best they can with the circumstances they've found themselves in, and have generously agreed to share their own personal journeys, and how they learned to step back at times and to step up at others. Their insights and reflections provide possible pathways to those already in similar circumstances, and to those about to embark on similar journeys.

The Fourteen Stories

Moira Rayner

A Social Justice Warrior in the Fight of Her Life

Moira Rayner is best remembered in Victoria as its last independent Commissioner for Equal Opportunity. She has also been Acting Deputy Director (Research) of the Australian Institute of Family Studies, a Hearings Commissioner of the Australian Human Rights Commission, an acting Corruption and Crime Commissioner and a full-time consultant in the national law firm now known as Norton Rose Fulbright, where for six years she helped establish the firm's Discrimination Law Practice, and worked with major employers, universities and government departments. She has been in-house senior legal counsel to Salmat Limited, and operates her successful management consultancy (Moira Rayner & Associates) and a small industrial law practice.

In 2000 she became the first Director of the Office of Children's Rights Commissioner for London, which modelled effective children's participation in government and is now an integral part of the Greater London Authority, London's regional government. She has co-authored several books on governance, human rights, children's participation, government policy and women and power (the latter with Joan Kirner). She hopes to finish her PhD (children's participation in public decision-making in Australia) by the end of this year.

In her spare time she volunteers as a solicitor with the Fitzroy Legal Service, serves on the Ethics Committee of Walter and Eliza Hall Institute, and sings in a small choir. She lives in Melbourne.

'I live because I am a Warrior and because I wish one day to be in the company of [She] for whom I have fought so hard.'
— John Bunyan

Actions have consequences

> *Question: What do you get when you mix a formidable, determined, outspoken woman with a powerful, conservative group of men hell-bent on revenge?*
>
> *Answer: A catastrophe of gigantic proportions that changed the course of this woman's life forever.*

This most Australian of stories starts with mateship — a compassionate visit to an old friend in hospital who was dying of cancer that led to immense and life-changing consequences.

What happened after Moira Rayner's hospital visit to Laurie Marquet became the subject of intense scrutiny, leading the police and the Western Australian Corruption and Crime Commission (WACCC) to pursue Moira for corruption and perverting the course of justice. If proven guilty, her stellar legal career would be in ruins.

How did she get into the situation where she misrepresented herself? She was a woman with a reputation for impeccable integrity, one of the country's most prominent and respected lawyers in the human rights and social justice landscape for decades. She had returned to Perth from London to care for her dying father, and had taken on the role of Assistant Commissioner for the WACCC,[1] which seemed like a pragmatic move for a 'social justice warrior' like Moira.

Things got complicated when her long-term friend Laurie, the Western Australian Clerk of Parliaments, became a person of interest to the WACCC. He was under investigation for drug possession and trafficking, and stealing money from parliament. He was also dying and in palliative care at a hospice. Despite warnings from the Corruption and Crime Commissioner (CCC) that visiting Laurie could put her in a compromising position, Moira visited her friend out of loyalty and compassion, as he was severely depressed and in need of comfort. She knew of his early background as a Redemptorist monk, and that he had made a suicide attempt years earlier when he had felt disgraced. She assured the CCC that she would not compromise herself and simply wanted to help Laurie 'make a good death'.

Unbeknown to Moira, Laurie's hospital room had been bugged and she was recorded warning him not to use his mobile phone. The response from some members of the Commission was fast and furious, and Moira found herself on the wrong side of a corruption investigation.

Moira has always been a fighter for social justice. A formidable opponent, you would want her in your corner, not your opponent's. She describes herself as a 'prickly' person, but possesses a big heart and is fiercely loyal to family and friends. She's outspoken and gutsy, yet shows great empathy towards victims, and though she's proud she's never arrogant. She is single-minded about standing up for the battler whose rights have been trampled on, irrespective of the political winds blowing at the time.

At times, these qualities meant Moira courted controversy. In 1994 her position was abolished by the Kennett government when, as Victoria's independent Human Rights and Equal Opportunity Commissioner, she advocated for women prisoners, defying the government's position on closing down Fairlea Women's prison and relocating the prisoners to Jika Jika Division in Pentridge, the high security wing of the men's prison, which had been declared unfit for human habitation in the 1980s.

Moira's predicament with the Commission ten years later may have been the direct result of her leveraging her very best qualities — empathy, compassion, loyalty and love.

The makings of a warrior

Moira says she was drawn towards representing the powerless in society from a very early age. Born in New Zealand to a very observant Protestant family, she was the second in a family of three children. Armed with strong guiding principles, she emerged from the back of the pack with a big, bold and controversial career, doing things on her own terms. Commencing her legal career as a generalist, she later specialised in Family Law before moving into a human rights advocacy role. She chaired the Law Reform Commission in Western Australia, was Commissioner for Equal Opportunity in Victoria, a Hearings Commissioner for the Australian Human Rights and Equal Opportunity Commission, and Director of the Office of the Children's Rights Commissioner for London. This last position was her dream job, which she had to abandon prematurely to care for her ill father in Perth. She then took on the fateful role of Acting Commissioner with the Western Australian Corruption and Crime Commission.

What lies beneath

To many of Moira's supporters, it was a mystery how this situation escalated to the point it did. It almost appeared to be some sort of witch-hunt, blown out of proportion. Moira believes there was a concerted effort to destroy her career by certain men in the powerful conservative establishment of Perth who harboured great enmity towards her. The seeds of dissent, Moira believes, stemmed from a strong dislike of her as an outspoken, prickly, loud and fiercely independent woman in a male-dominated establishment. There had also been an earlier confrontation at the Commission that she believes set some of her colleagues against her. In a nutshell, a senior staff member deliberately disobeyed her instructions and, when found out, was ordered by the Commissioner to apologise. Moira believes the loss of face for this powerful individual, and the acrimony the incident caused, set a climate of hostility and revenge that she could have avoided with a wiser approach.

Whatever the motivation, the situation looked grim. Phone taps can be used to devastating effect when selectively played in court. Moira's accusers claimed she warned Laurie that the Commission was monitoring his calls. She states they selectively used recorded conversations to 'stitch her up'. She says she simply advised him to look after himself in his final days and prepare to die in peace. In fact she had called the Commissioner the day after her first visit and told him that Laurie might well be prepared to make a dying declaration and clear his conscience before he died, if the Commissioner felt able to visit himself.

The public response was shrill and remorseless. Western Australian Attorney General Jim McGinty described Moira's actions as 'shocking, inappropriate, intolerable, appalling and disturbing' and her behaviour as 'unconscionable'.[2] Radio station host Paul Murray accused her of being a Labor mate who didn't deserve the job. 'She's a bleeding-heart leftie,' he said, 'and I would have expected her to react [to Laurie] that way, which is why she shouldn't have been in the job in the first place.'[3] Moira says some sections of the media went too far. The paparazzi staked out her father's house, which was highly distressing to her dying father and herself. Using funds raised by the Friends of Moira, she and her legal team fought the charges to the bitter end. After a waiting period of more than a year and a trial lasting two and a half days, one charge (of 'corruption') was withdrawn, and the court eventually acquitted her of attempting to pervert the course of justice. But by that stage the damage to her career had been done, not to mention the personal toll it took on Moira and her family. Her father died within weeks of her being charged. Some of her enemies camped in the back of the courtroom and were visibly furious at her acquittal, she said.

In the slough of despond

The slough of despond is a deep swamp in John Bunyan's allegory *The Pilgrim's Progress*, into which the protagonist Christian sinks under the weight of his sins and his sense of guilt for them. He can only pull himself out of the swamp by reaching out and grasping the hand of a friend prepared to rescue him. Moira uses this analogy to describe how despairing she felt during this time.

Experiencing one significant event can be highly stressful, but multiple events can be catastrophic to one's health and wellbeing. In Moira's situation, there was a 'perfect storm', where a string of events collided. Between August 2005 and the trial in November 2006, Moira had to weather the accusations and media storm, and resigned. Two months later the charges of being corrupt and perverting the course of justice were laid. She had to deal with her father's death and her mother's illness, experienced the death of another close family member, had to deal with an ongoing barrage of public abuse and accusations, and chose to relocate back to Melbourne, returning only to farewell her father nearly a year before the trial and acquittal. Two weeks after she was exonerated, her mother died in her arms. Moira describes this time as the closest she ever got to a nervous breakdown.

> *'It was an absolute nightmare ... I was shattered when two charges were laid, not just attempting to pervert the course of justice but also corruption, which was absurd but nonetheless it actually kicked me in the guts. I was feeling terrible anyway and I started to doubt my own sanity, my recollection of events ... I was beset, anxious, dreadfully worried about my father and my mother — thinking I'd just disgraced and upset everybody that I loved. That was far more worrying than anything else, as a matter of fact. I also felt terribly misunderstood.'*

What was I thinking?

Moira speaks of acting out some rather 'bizarre behaviour' and making several poorly judged decisions she would not have made under normal circumstances. Her first instincts were to look out for Laurie's soul, unaware that her own situation was about to get more precarious than his. She contacted several friends and spiritual guides, including the Archbishop of Perth, in the hope that they might visit Laurie and minister comfort to him. Even this most well-meaning action, she says, took on sinister undertones, being interpreted by her accusers as an attempt to send in a rescue party and avoid having him charged. Another poor decision was speaking to the media when she should have stayed silent. Friends were aghast at her inaccurate recollections of that time; 'That's not at all what happened,' she remembers them saying on several occasions. '[One friend] thought I was barking mad because I was so anxious for Laurie's soul, when actually I was in the firing line and Laurie was going to die anyway.'

This was a period where Moira was incapable of focusing her mind on anything other than her predicament. Returning to work was just not possible at that time.

Some psychotherapists and neuroscientists would recognise these behaviours as the manifestations of 'amygdala hijack', a term first coined by Daniel Goleman.[4] Under stress all our effort and attention fixates on the event or incident that's upsetting, frustrating, or angering us. In this state our memory reprioritises what it pays attention to so that whatever relates to the perceived threat comes to mind most readily and we lose the ability to think clearly, balance emotions and have perspective. Plus, we tend to fall back on habits and responses learned early in life — which can lead to impulsive, irrational and destructive responses that we regret later and lead us astray.

So where did the helping hand come from, the one that pulled Moira out of the swamp of despair? After some soul-searching and after hearing the Director of the Campion Centre of Ignatian Spirituality in Melbourne, she realised her personal journey back to living an authentic life and understanding her purpose would be found in the structured processes of meditation and mindfulness practiced through the St Ignatian spiritual exercises.[5] Through this practice Moira was at last able to pause and reflect on her circumstances, gain clarity of direction and return to living her core values and purpose. She still takes great strength from the Ignatian structure of daily life, book-ending her days with meditation and reflection.

> *'At the end of 36 weeks of daily meditations and exercises I learned how your imagination can be used to give you insight into your current situation ... and sort out what your relationships were with other people. I had a sense of purpose. I came out of it clear about who I was, where I got the biggest charge. And oddly enough, it was working with vulnerable groups, particularly children, but also the people I have been giving advice to at the Fitzroy Legal Service.'*

Research on mindfulness supports this outcome.[6] Focusing the mind through meditation enables us to create a gap between impulse and action, giving us the ability to make more informed choices, rather than being swept away by our first impulses.

Getting back on the horse

Giving up was never on Moira's radar. She muses on resilience in a somewhat paradoxical way — something that can be cultivated in life, but also eroded if left unattended. An attack on resilience is like an attack on a tree with an axe, says Moira: the tree may survive but often it becomes deformed after the attack. If the roots survive the tree continues to grow, but it will never be the same again. Moira is still the same person, but changed in ways she never imagined.

It helped having friends with the courage to speak candidly about what they were seeing and hearing. The generous financial support from Friends of Moira for her legal fees also humbled and sustained her.

Returning to work was also cathartic. During the 16 months between the charges laid and the acquittal, Moira returned to Melbourne to get her life back in order, and consulted for a time with the firm Diversity at Work. Returning to a solo legal practice was a natural step for her, like putting on a comfortable pair of shoes that have been nicely worn in. She now manages two businesses: her own legal practice and a human resources consultancy.

Reflections

Alongside co-author of *The Women's Power Handbook*, the late former Victorian Premier Joan Kirner, Moira put together the 'Top Ten Assets for Successful Women',[7] a set of guiding principles for empowering women. Moira reflects on how each of them may have worked in practice through this crisis.

1. A clear sense of purpose	'I'd made plenty of mistakes. The most important one was losing my sense of purpose. Without a sense of purpose it's very easy to be knocked off your even keel.' Once she regained her purpose through meditation, it became her beacon for redirecting her career.
2. Confidence	'Smashed. I had to rebuild it.'
3. Integrity, underpinned by values	'I'm very clear about my own integrity, and I don't think I did a damn thing at that time which was other than stupid. However, I spoke the truth to people who were malevolent.'
4. Community/ team focus	'That's the one that hurt most — my rejection by the legal community, that people thought of me as a "rat bag" and someone you could [abuse] in the street.'
5. Information	'I wasn't taking anything in.'
6. Balance and common sense	'Went out the door.'
7. Self-knowledge and discipline	'That's what I was working on — to regain.'
8. Imagination	'I'd lost imaginative contemplation and regained it through a familiar but long-forgotten practice of meditation and prayer.'
9. A sense of humour	'Totally lost.'
10. Humanity	About the conflict in the Commission: 'Instead of showing that I was upset and asking for assurances, I could have been nice … and made him a cup of tea, and there's nothing wrong with that. He went out furious.'

Lessons learned

Moira's personal insights come from a deep place of hard-learned wisdom. Turning her experiences into pragmatic advice to other women, she offers seven key pieces of advice:

1. *Never lose your sense of purpose.* Never deviate from what you understand to be your purpose, not just in your career, but in life. Without a sense of purpose, you lose direction and sever connection to your values.
2. *Bring people along with you.* 'If there's something that needs to be done, taking people with you is always better than trying to do it on your own. I'd forgotten my own advice,' Moira recalls. She strongly believes had she handled the situation of conflict with a senior staff member of the Commission prior to the hospital visit differently — in a spirit of forgiveness rather than conflict — the situation could have been avoided if she had been both tactful and empathetic.
3. *Cover yourself.* Moira's biggest mistake, she says, was not the fact that she visited Laurie, but that she went there alone. Had she taken a colleague or another witness to the hospice who could have vouched for her on that day and the other drop-in visit she made the following week, she believes things might have turned out very differently. But by then the seeds of revenge and retaliation had been sown, and she feels she was led into a trap, partly due to her own naivety.
4. *Know when to remain silent.* Moira says she spoke at times, intending to clear her name, when she should have stayed silent. This includes speaking to the media ('stupid', she says), and speaking candidly and forcefully to a hostile audience, when she should have been circumspect.
5. *Don't avoid conflict.* Do the best you can, look at every angle of the conflict or situation before deciding to fight or walk away.

However, know that your judgment, no matter how you feel about it, is being badly affected.

6. *Assess the situation objectively.* There's no escaping stress; effectively handling it is the key. Ignatius offers several methods for objectively assessing a situation that will help you gain clarity about the right direction to take. Here are four of them:
    a. Write down a list of advantages and disadvantages for each course of action. Leave the list alone for a while, then return to it.
    b. Put yourself into a third-person position. What advice would you give someone who was in a similar situation to you and came to you for advice?
    c. Imagine you have a fatal illness and only 12 months to live. You are now at that point 12 months later and looking back. Imagine what you are looking at, what you thought then and what you think now.
    d. Commence a practice of constant reflection as a daily discipline. Reflect on what's happening now, what's working and not working, how the day will go, what you'll do tomorrow.
7. *Find a confidante* — someone you can trust unconditionally, who has no vested interest in your success, and who knows nothing about your professional life. This person will give you perspective and help you work out the right approach. Remember that many personal friends who have your best interests at heart will give you advice that's well intentioned, but not necessarily wise.

Moira seems to have found her own rhythm now, after what could be described as her 'time in the wilderness'. She has fought, regrouped, and re-emerged with a renewed sense of purpose. Though the scars of the battle may remain, there is clarity and certainty about each day and the work she now chooses to take on.

Her Excellency Frances Adamson

A Trailblazer

Her Excellency Frances Adamson has been Australia's Ambassador to the People's Republic of China since August 2011. She has twice served in the Australian High Commission in London, as Deputy High Commissioner from 2005 to 2008 and Political Counsellor from 1993 to 1997. She was Chief of Staff to the Minister for Foreign Affairs and then the Minister for Defence from 2009 to 2010.

Frances is an honorary patron of the China-Australia Chamber of Commerce in Beijing, patron of the Australia-China Alumni Association, a member of the Advisory Board of the Australian National University's Australian Centre on China in the World, an ex-officio member of the Leadership Council of the Australia-China Youth Dialogue, and a director of China Matters Ltd, a not-for-profit organisation established to raise awareness in Australia of the changes in China's society, economy and polity.

She is married to Rod Bunten. They have four children, and both speak Mandarin Chinese.

Ambassador Frances Adamson breaks new ground around what it means to be a woman leader. She epitomises that rare combination of a woman who takes charge and takes care, is highly competent and is liked.[1] Her career story is characterised by diligence, hard work and sound planning, underpinned by a preparedness to back herself.

Who is Ambassador Frances Adamson?

Frances Adamson is a sixth-generation South Australian whose forebears on both sides of the family were early settlers, on the land in the mid-north of the state and in Adelaide. Maternal and paternal grandfathers conducted businesses in or near the city, and both families made sacrifices to send their children to private schools.

Strong women's voices of authority and learning were part and parcel of Frances's upbringing, surrounded by her grandmother, mother and numerous aunts, not to mention her high-achieving younger sister, Christine Adamson, a New South Wales Supreme Court judge. Her father, Ian Adamson, was a management consultant and general manager of several businesses, and her brother Stuart is an Anglican Chaplain at the Prince of Wales Hospital in Sydney. Frances recalls that growing up in a family with a mother as a Member of Parliament instilled in her a sense of service to the community — not that it crossed her mind at that stage to follow in her mother's footsteps.

No doubt the discussions held around the dining table would have been wide ranging and stimulating, helping shape her views about life, politics and discovering her place in the world. Little wonder, then, that Frances was well equipped to take charge of her life and develop into the leader she has become.

An accidental diplomat

In 1979, Frances spent 12 months in the Netherlands on an AFS scholarship, and a couple of years later backpacked around Europe with her younger sister. She returned to Adelaide to complete her economics degree, but decided to discontinue studies in law. Of her experience in the Netherlands, Frances recalls:

> *'That whole environment, even though it was a European-centric one, opened my mind to what was going on in the world — to the legacies of the Second World War, to the Soviet Union stationing missiles, President Jimmy Carter in the United States. I got back to Adelaide University, and I remember standing outside the library waiting for it to open — it was my one real experience of reverse culture shock because I'd been in this rich environment — and I heard other students on the steps of the library talking about Carter. I thought they were talking about Jimmy Carter, and I went closer and it turned out they were talking about a South Australian footballer.'*

A passion for world affairs was kindled, which would inexorably lead to her starting a career in Canberra. She wasn't initially attracted to Canberra — she had experienced it as a somewhat boring city in her youth — until she was introduced to a number of key policy-makers through the 'Economists in Action' scheme, a government-sponsored initiative for final year economics students. She then realised that interesting work could be done within the hallowed walls of government and perhaps she could be part of it.

When offered a traineeship at the Department of Foreign Affairs (DFA, later Department of Foreign Affairs and Trade — DFAT) upon graduating, the idea of becoming a diplomat had her in its grip. She ditched other offers, as well as her plans to continue with an Honours year, to seize this opportunity.

A life of firsts

Her potential as a leader was apparent from her university days. In 1984 she became the first female captain of the Adelaide University Boat Club, with more than a century of male captains before her.

She joined DFA in 1985, the year after the Sex Discrimination Act was passed. For some years DFA had attracted roughly equal numbers of men and women applicants, but until then the men had tended to take the lion's share of appointments. As a result of the Sex Discrimination Act the department reviewed its hiring policies and, for the first time in DFA's history, 14 women and 12 men were selected. She reminisces about that time, when she and other women keenly felt questions being levelled at them around tokenism and not being appointed on merit. It didn't last more than a few months — perhaps a salient lesson for today's debate around gender quotas and perceptions of fairness.

Five years later, when she married Rod Bunten, a UK diplomat, having dual diplomatic careers was unusual — almost always, the wife had a different career or gave up her career to support her husband.

In 2001 she was appointed Australia's first female Head of Post in Taipei. She and Rod were the first dual career 'diplomatic couple' there, with Rod the British Deputy Head of Post. At first, she says, the Taiwanese were concerned about how they could each do their jobs without breaking confidences involving both countries' relations with Taiwan. By the end of their posting they were asked to speak of their experiences to Taiwanese diplomats, as an example of how it was possible to maintain dual careers in the diplomatic service. Frances and Rod both declined, not wanting to be cast as a 'diplomatic freak show'.

The couple were a curiosity in Taipei for other reasons. Frances recalls Taiwanese children turning to watch them walking with their blonde-haired children, and counting them with some surprise because there were so many — one, two, three, four! Not that this impacted on her work in any way — if anything, it could have been a positive distinguishing feature, Frances muses.

Similarly, in China in 2011, Frances was Australia's first woman Ambassador. While there were over 160 Ambassadors, a scant ten percent or so were women. Having four children in a country with a one-child policy also turned heads. Frances plays down the impact of being the first: 'It's a fact, nothing more than that,' she says.

Planning diligently for success, with a bit of good timing

Frances's story of success has not always been a smooth ride. After she and Rod decided to be together, they approached their working lives in the spirit of true partnership, committed to maintaining both of their careers. They took a year to hammer out a plan that would work. First, Rod would take a year of unpaid leave in Australia while Frances worked on the Taiwan desk. They would then both return to London, where Frances would look for work with the High Commission. Then it would be back to Canberra, seek a posting together in a third country, and let the future take care of itself.

All went to plan, except for the uncertainty at the outset about Frances taking unpaid leave to head to London, as a fairly junior diplomat at the time. The only certain way of getting unpaid leave was for her to take maternity leave. So it seemed logical to bring forward their plans to start a family. Their first child, Claire, was born in September 1991 after they had both been in Canberra for a year. Frances joined Rod in London a few weeks after he returned there, in a cold one-bedroom flat 'in the wrong end of Wimbledon', experiencing her first UK winter.

Despite all this planning, a bit of luck along the way helped. When she felt ready to go back to work in London, a colleague arranged for her to be introduced to the Australian High Commissioner at a time when they needed someone to develop their workplace diversity program — a perfect three-day-a-week role for her. Towards the end of this assignment, the Australian Foreign Minister, Gareth Evans, had asked DFAT to develop a program of short-term overseas missions that would be offered first to women on maternity leave as a way to optimise their productivity. As a result, in September 1992, Frances was offered an outstanding opportunity to go to the United Nations in New York, working in the Australian Permanent Mission during the annual session of the United Nations General Assembly.

Staring into the abyss

Both parents loved being with Claire, of course. Frances says, 'She had us wrapped around her little finger from day one.'

In the three months or so that Frances had moved to London, she had made friends with some other women with children around the same age. However, being in London without family was tough. Her mother had been there for her in Australia — and has subsequently supported her for several weeks after the birth of all of her children — and life as a mother was very different to life as an energetic rising star in the diplomatic world. There came a time when Frances couldn't see a clear way to return to the workforce.

'It was pretty grim,' she recalls, 'it was a big contrast from where I'd come from.' Becoming immersed in a child's world was a wonderful thing, but it was different to the adult world. She loved being a mother, but worried that there was no certainty of being able to return to work. She concluded she must have sent out distress signals in some way, because suddenly she was receiving letters and phone calls from family and friends concerned about her.

It was time to take charge. She arranged for a friend to look after Claire and headed to the Australian High Commission to introduce herself and ask for part-time work.

She wasn't going back to work for the money. She recalls that by the time she had paid the part-time nanny, bought public transport fares and a few personal items, she was left with about £10 a week. But getting back to work was an essential part of who she was, and having a nanny was an investment in the future if she decided to have more children.

Frances was back and she relished it: 'I loved going up to Waterloo on the train, crossing the bridge on the bus, walking in to Australia House, and just doing something interesting and meaningful and different from what I'd done before.'

She'd had 18 months maternity leave and going back to full-time work after such a long period would be the most difficult of all her maternity leave break decisions. She felt vulnerable. How would she go? Could she still do what she had been able to 18 months ago? How would it work with the new baby? The longer she was away from work the larger these concerns seemed to loom.

Part of the solution lay in high-quality, reliable childcare; a live-in Australian nanny for each of the first two years and then Victoria, a wonderful British nanny, who became part of the family for longer than anyone imagined.

Making it work

While seen as high-achieving, Frances was not someone likely to prioritise work advancement over family obligations. Being well equipped to take charge, she and Rod planned as much as they could, leaving some room for flexibility when needed.

From her earliest years, family was integral to Frances. As a daughter of a politician and prominent Member of Parliament, she understood the stresses and challenges facing mothers who combined a challenging calling with motherhood. She recalls going on the campaign trail with her mother when she was seeking pre-selection. Like many women politicians, she had been pre-selected to a marginal seat, so campaigning required complete dedication, and once she won the seat the pressures would have been enormous.

Frances says her mother successfully hid the extreme pressures and long hours from the children — they really had no idea when Mum didn't come home until the early hours of the morning. The important thing was that she was there when they needed her. This background would have fortified her for the challenges of work and family life when her turn came.

After each child was born, Frances's mother would support her for at least two weeks. She would be up every night with Frances, feeding and cleaning, just being there to ease the heavy burden.

The shape of the day was created around Claire and the other children: 'There's nothing like the visual image of a child standing, nose pressed against a window at seven o'clock at night, waiting for you to walk in the door, to make sure that you finish doing what you're doing.'

Right from the start, Frances had set herself a firm rule:

> *'I would work at work, and home would be home. As soon as I walked in the door I'd stop thinking about work, and as soon as I walked in the door at work I'd stop thinking about home. It seemed to me not productive to feel guilty in both places, and this way I was able to throw myself into each part of it.'*

A typical evening at home would have gone something like the following. The children would have been fed and bathed before Rod and Frances got home, and would be waiting for stories, read by Frances when they were little and Rod as they grew older. Rod or Victoria would cook dinner and the three adults would eat together, catching up on the children's doings. Time with her children was very special for Frances.

She had to be resourceful, creative and flexible around prioritising family and work commitments. For example, when offered the short-term mission to New York, her brother kindly agreed to come to New York to look after Claire. Family to the rescue! Accommodation was to be provided in a hotel room, but by demonstrating that a less central two-bedroom apartment would be cheaper, a workable solution was found.

Stable childcare arrangements were another non-negotiable rule, and having a live-in nanny made even more sense after they had their third child. They were fortunate to have Victoria with them for 13 years, a nanny who travelled everywhere with them and was a major part of the lives of the whole family. She recalls they were absolutely like-minded about parenting.

Working in an office had its own challenges, especially when she was breastfeeding. She remembers excruciating pain in the first few weeks, especially after her second child, Matthew, but was insistent on continuing to breastfeed. She saw it as a way of returning to work and maintaining a bond with each of the children. Psychologically, knowing she was supplying milk for them was very important. Thank goodness for the breast pump!

In Canberra she had a lock installed on her office door to avoid embarrassment. It's there to this day, and she's sure not many people know what it's for. She recalls a Deputy Secretary rattling on her door once, wondering why it was locked, calling out, 'Frances, are you in there?'

'Yes,' she replied, 'I'll be with you in a moment.'

'Is it something to do with your baby?' he asked.

'Yes, it is,' was the answer.

Later, before her posting to Taipei, she became known for having 'Sophie breaks'. Sophie, their fourth child, was only four months old when Frances prepared to move to Taipei. A morning 'Sophie break' and an afternoon 'Sophie break' were scheduled into her diary in order for Frances to breastfeed her. Between these breaks she would be calling on a premier, minister, cultural organisation, businessperson or doing a media interview.

Although the basic home and work arrangements were in place, it was still tough, especially when the children were sick. Her third child, Katherine, needed special attention. She had what the paediatrician determined to be low muscle tone, which meant she was delayed in hitting her milestones and needed physiotherapy, occupational therapy and speech therapy over the years. These unscheduled needs had to be factored in to the couple's day. Rod was always supportive, and Frances had an extraordinary boss who backed her all the way and gave her the flexibility she needed to be able to attend to family responsibilities.

Despite the juggling, long hours and constant tiredness, Frances possessed an ability to seem calm, highly capable and in control at work. She remembers a performance appraisal where her boss commended her on a strong year of high performance. She was flabbergasted by this perception and responded: 'I've been crazed with tiredness, I haven't been able to really do what I could have done before; I'm just hanging on.'

From early in their marriage, Frances and Rod divided the responsibilities. Rod agreed to do the cooking and 'turned it into an art form'. For Frances, family meals have always been very important, not just for the food but for the interaction between family members.

Frances does, however, feel she got the lion's share of the nappy changing, something she resented from time to time. But then Rod took on extra responsibilities as the children grew older, taking them to museums and zoos, and introducing them to books and games. Parenting became a completely shared enterprise.

With her moves into more senior roles, the balance between work and family became harder to manage. This was particularly acute when in 2008 the Minister for Foreign Affairs, Stephen Smith, approached her to become his Chief of Staff. Her immediate reaction was that while this was a role she had aspired to, with four children aged between eight and 18, and with Rod by then undertaking teacher training, she wouldn't be able to fulfil the role if it involved being available 24 hours a day.

Where there is a will, however, there is a way. Frances agreed to take the role on very specific conditions: she needed to be home by 7pm each night in non-sitting weeks of parliament, and she would restrict her travel, especially to Perth and overseas, only to those times when she felt she could add value. The Minister agreed, and by and large these conditions were met.

Of course, Frances and Rod had to deal with crises as they arose, but they could also call on reinforcements, such as Victoria the nanny, and family who were mostly on hand. Also, with a ten-year gap between their oldest and youngest child, the older ones were increasingly able to help.

They decided early on to keep the children with them for as long as possible, rather than send them to boarding school. This ensured they could retain the close bond they cherished. It wasn't until the children started to get into the complications of the last two years of school, Years 11 and 12, that they had to contemplate boarding school. It was better for the children to board at a school rather than continue to travel with their parents, which would have been too much of an upheaval during those important years. Claire spent her last two and a half years of school at a boarding school in Australia. Matthew chose to go to Beijing and attend an international school. Katherine chose to complete Years 11 and 12 in Australia. Sophie, their youngest, is currently completing her last year of middle school.

What about nurturing the relationship between Rod and herself? Each Thursday was date night, and once a year they would take a weekend away together. At the time of writing this book, the couple were about to return to Hong Kong to celebrate their 25th wedding anniversary.

You did what?

How many women would have the boldness to apply for a promotion while they were on maternity leave? Well Frances did, twice, and was successful on both occasions.

The first time was towards the middle of her first period of maternity leave, with Claire. She applied for promotion to the diplomatic rank of Counsellor, one level up from her then level of First Secretary. She remembers being delighted just to have the opportunity of a telephone interview that occurred in the kitchen of Rod's little flat in Wimbledon. Rod had taken Claire out, the place was piled high with dishes and she had notes stuck up on the walls. She remembers getting through the interview and concluding to herself that she'd done abysmally. Perhaps that vulnerability she spoke about earlier was showing through. She recalls:

> *'We were due to drive to Dover that day and go across the channel to have a holiday in France. I think I spent the whole trip to Dover telling Rod how badly I'd done, and that I'd never been promoted and I'd never get this proper long-term posting in London.'*

She did get promoted, finally obtaining the long-term posting in London they had planned for years ago, and still doesn't know how.

The second time she applied for a promotion was after the birth of her third child, Katherine, in 1997. This was a big step up into the Senior Executive Service. She negotiated a delayed starting date so she could spend more time with her children before taking on the challenging new role, returning to work after five months maternity leave. She was promoted again before departing for Taipei and recalls, 'I'd just been appointed to my first Head of Post role with a six-month-old baby, four children and a working husband in a different mission. That was pretty tough.'

Sacrifices

As the couple approached the 20-year mark of juggling both their careers and their relationship, it became apparent that it was becoming harder to manage joint careers. The pressures on the family and their lives while juggling two diplomatic careers, especially synchronising two relocations every time, was becoming too difficult. After much discussion it was Rod who decided to sacrifice his Foreign Service career.

Rod decided to return to his first love — physics — and retrained as a physics teacher. The idea was that this would be a skill that would be usable anywhere in the world. However, having found teaching in Canberra even more enjoyable and rewarding than expected, he finds himself frustrated at not being permitted — for visa reasons — to teach in Beijing.

Insights

Every family circumstance is different and there is no one right way to arrange your work and family commitments. However, here are some suggestions that can be gleaned from the Adamson-Bunten family experience:

- What Frances didn't tell me outright, but I gleaned from her story, was this: it is important to be excellent at your job as the foundation for everything else. If you are a high performer you will be sought after, and this gives you leverage and a certain amount of power to ask for what you need.

- Understand what is most important in your life and put in place routines and rules to protect those elements.
- Be flexible. Concentrate on what is most important and leave the rest for later. You don't have to be perfect at everything.
- Have support systems in place — a partner who is fully on board with your career, a nanny, housekeeper, cleaner, gardener, whatever you need and whatever you can afford. Think about the cost as an investment in the long-term success of your career and your family life.
- Plan for what can go wrong. Have contingencies in place. Having family or reliable friends on hand can help enormously in times of crisis.
- Keep connected while you are away from work. Retaining a profile in the workplace will remind key decision-makers of your value to the organisation, and will make it easier to negotiate a successful return to a role you want on your terms.
- Back yourself. Go for promotions. Go for what others don't expect you to. Request flexibility when you need it. If you don't ask for it, you won't get it!
- Work for a caring and understanding boss who will advocate for you. Policies and procedures around parental leave and flexibility are simply the baseline. How they are implemented is hugely dependent on a boss who 'gets it' and will ensure the flexibility you need will work for you and the organisation.
- Work for an organisation where flexibility and time away from the office is accepted as the norm. Workplaces where 'face time in the office' is regarded as all-important puts you at a disadvantage when you take extended periods of leave.

Dr Helen Szoke

So Much More than a Job

Dr Helen Szoke is a human rights advocate who has worked for many years to stop race discrimination in Australia, and who is passionate and vocal about women's rights and gender equality in Australia and around the world.

Helen commenced as Chief Executive of Oxfam Australia in January 2013. Prior to this appointment, she served as Australia's Federal Race Discrimination Commissioner, following seven years as the Victorian Equal Opportunity and Human Rights Commissioner.

Helen is currently an appointed member of the C20 advisory group and Co-Chair of Make Poverty History. She is an Executive Committee member of the Australian Council For International Development (ACFID) and the ACFID Humanitarian Reference Group (HRG) Champion. Helen is a member of the Deakin University Master of International and Community Development Advisory Board, and sits on the Executive Board of Oxfam International.

In 2011 Helen was awarded the Law Institute of Victoria Paul Baker Award for her contribution to human rights. In 2014 she received the University of Melbourne Alumni Award for leadership. Helen has extensive experience in management, community development, organisational development, consumer advocacy and regulation in the education and health sectors. She is a graduate of the Australian Institute of Company Directors and a fellow of the Institute of Public Administration.

'I still have my feet on the ground, I just wear better shoes.'
— Oprah Winfrey

From her early days in the housing commission flats of Smithton in North West Tasmania, Helen Szoke has emerged to become one of the most influential leading women in shaping public policy on key social issues.

Walking in to Helen's office, I get the distinct impression of a woman who is determined, thriving and on top of her game — she is professionally assured, focused, has her diary organised to within an inch of its life and has the office running like a well-oiled machine. But her life hasn't always run so smoothly. She has pulled herself out of a tough and underprivileged childhood, and has experienced personal hardship along the way. She understands how chaotic life can be when juggling professional success with personal achievement, all the while bringing up a brood of five children and also engaged with three stepchildren.

Although tertiary qualified, Helen has always had her feet firmly planted on the ground. Some of her most important education came from life's experiences, the kind they don't teach you at university.

A migrant success story that crumbled

As with all of us, Helen's childhood and life experiences have had a profound influence on her character and decisions as an adult. Her father came to Australia from Hungary in the postwar period as a refugee. His business success in Australia descended into poverty in the 1960s when Australia went into a brief recession, marked by soaring inflation, large job losses and a credit squeeze. To keep their heads above water the family decided to move to Tasmania. Helen recalls the stigma of being a poor migrant living in a housing commission area with other low-income families, with a father who worked for a mining company and a mother who remained at home.

Prior to this, at six years of age, Helen and her sister were adopted 'as a set'. She was determined that this experience was not going to define her life, driven by a very competitive streak. She was certain about where she was headed, with a sense that 'I'm going to rise above this and be really good at what I do'.

A defining moment came with the election of the Whitlam government and the abolition of university fees. Recognising that education was the path out of poverty, she completed an Arts Degree at the University of Tasmania. She became quite politicised through the social, environmental and political debates raging through the universities during this era. This period awoke in her an awareness of the social change that can be achieved through government intervention.

Indebted to her difficult start in life

Growing up among the battlers provided Helen with a great empathy for the struggles facing disadvantaged families. She recognised that the circumstances that create poverty in the first place are often based around significant economic, political and social factors rather than caused by personal failings or poor decisions — and that more than individual will is required to achieve lasting social change. Her parents taught her that having the privilege of a university education meant she had a responsibility to do something with it. These teachings strongly influenced her as she grew, and have guided how she has lived her life ever since.

Career serendipity

There appears to be no careful plan to her career, Helen says, but you don't get to be an Equal Opportunity Commissioner, a Race Discrimination Commissioner, and then a CEO of one of Australia's most influential non-government organisations (NGOs) by accident.

Two key themes emerge from Helen's career: community and people. She possesses a strong understanding of what makes communities strong and leverages this in all her roles. She has great empathy, understands people and where they are coming from, and meets them there. Her mission has always been to shape public opinion and policy on key social issues, and achieves this to get the best outcome for more vulnerable communities. These themes have both consciously and unconsciously driven her career choices.

> *'I started at the community and learnt the kind of principles of community development and social justice, and then could apply those through everything else I've done.'*

On graduating from university, Helen shifted to the 'mainland' and began a career as a Community Education Officer for the Victorian Education Department.

She had her first child at 29, but the relationship ended four months after his birth. Helen became a single mother, and learned first-hand about the juggling act of women who are primary carers and also trying to launch a successful career.

She returned to work when her first child was about six to eight months old, to a part-time position at a teacher's union. As a single mother she discovered the challenges of undertaking the responsibilities that two people would normally share, such as child drop-offs and pick-ups at childcare, financial responsibilities and managing sick children, not to mention needing to find the energy to spend time with her child at the end of the day.

> *'I really wanted to be a mother; I wanted to have a good relationship with my kids. I was willing to take the risk, no matter what the consequences, so I made it work.'*

Working in the community sector provided Helen with access to maternity leave and part-time work, which enabled her to carve out some measure of financial independence. She also worked in a predominantly young, female workforce, so managers had little option but to accommodate the needs of women juggling work and family responsibilities.

Helen remarried and acquired two beautiful stepchildren. She also had two children of her own in this marriage. All up, the household boasted five children.

While on maternity leave, Helen embarked on a consulting path for a time, leveraging her experience in the community sector. However, she struggled with the loneliness and isolation of consulting, and longed to return to a more interactive workplace. This is a challenge faced by many women, and Helen states she probably did not work it through as well as she could have. Notwithstanding, she accepted a role at the Royal Melbourne Hospital and the next stage of her career began. She project-managed the closure of the Royal Park Psychiatric Hospital — an enormous, demanding and complex role in transformational change.

On her own again — crazy times but full of fun

Being a mother on her own again was just as chaotic but somehow different the second time around. She was more mature, with more of life's experiences under her belt. Her career had taken off, so she was financially more secure. Also, she didn't have to do all the heavy lifting on her own.

However, managing the children was different. Her former husband was a highly engaged and dedicated father, determined to also care for the children after their marriage ended. The children were of different ages (between two years and 13 years old), could support each other, and were happy in each other's company. Also, there were economies of scale of having a larger family. They were a 'gun unit' together, Helen recalls. There was a lot of interaction, a synergy, and a kind of support system with five children that you don't have with one. Having a 'critical mass' of five children meant that hiring a nanny was a practical and logical decision — and having all those kids around was simply great fun, she recalls.

> *'The kids just tumbled all over each other all of the time, and we had to get out and make time for each other collectively and individually as mother and children. I think back on it now and wonder, "God, how did we ever cope?"'*

Working in the public sector meant Helen was able to take flexible hours — arrive late in the morning to help out at the children's school, leave to attend events or look after sick children and be involved in the Parents and Friends Association.

> *'If I was running my own business or another kind of business that placed a much greater demand on me being present and putting in the time, those things would have been a real conflict with what I wanted to be as a parent.'*

Success strategies

So how did Helen stay on an even keel? Honest communication was the key, reflects Helen, combined with understanding her limitations. With her children she was open about her feelings, plans and movements, and this honesty forged a strong bond that lasts until today, with the kids all grown up and with lives of their own.

She never felt miserable when she compared herself to other women who were perhaps on fixed hours, shift work, or working in client service for low wages. These women were tackling the same challenges and making it work in different ways, and compared to their circumstances she felt relatively lucky.

Helen is one of the most organised and productive women I've met. Despite this, she says she has never felt as though she 'lined up the ducks' and never really got to the point where she's had the situation 'nailed' — until the children were older, when a different relationship developed. In the days before technology such as the Blackberry, which enabled employees to work more flexibly, Helen recalls squeezing tasks into every moment of her day. When her role at the Royal Melbourne Hospital finished her staff wrote her a song, in which they recalled her using the Dictaphone in the car to and from picking up children, to and from work, whenever she could, to maximise her productivity.

Helen also possessed a strong measure of grit and self-confidence, and the optimism that she could manage it all. She just assumed she could have both a successful career and a successful family life, and she would do both:

> *'I wanted to have it all and I was going to make it happen. If that meant I had to be super organised or I had to negotiate something, or find support, then that's what I would do.'*

She learned to understand her limitations and her role as a stepmother — you don't have to be a mother to children who still have their own mother, she discovered. Yet she felt strongly that no matter what, she would always be there for them.

She describes her third biological child as 'rush proof' — she was so calm even going off to childcare:

> *'There was this whole machine above her coming and going and me trying to organise it, and she just managed her own way through.'*

Somehow she has always managed to make time for herself, such as keeping fit by going for a run or to the gym.

For the last 19 years she has also had the strong support of her husband, whose three children make up the number of children between them to eight. This kind of family is not easy and there are a lot of relationships to keep track of, but Helen says through it all he has backed her and given her the confidence to lift and build her career. She has also benefited from his expertise as an experienced businessman and Chief Executive.

Her children have given back in spades. She credits them with grounding her, with teaching her about the kind of world they want to inherit, and driving her to achieve that world for them and their own children. They have also given her confidence as a person, being so proud of their achievements and 'basking in their reflected glory'.

> *'The most important thing I've ever done in my life is have kids, and the thing I'm most proud of is my kids. They are doing amazing work around the world in very different ways, and the relationship is mutual — they are very proud of me.'*

The three-pieced jigsaw

Now that Helen is in a senior leadership role, she firmly believes that it's up to women like her and other leaders, both women and men, to do the heavy lifting on three key fronts: the workplace culture level, the regulatory level and the societal level. These three elements are like pieces of jigsaw that, when they fit snugly together, will create the kind of society that maximises the potential contribution of everyone and raises the productivity of the economy as a whole.

1. An inclusive and diverse workplace culture

First, leaders need to create diverse and inclusive cultures, where women and men can advance while bringing their whole selves to work. At Oxfam, Helen strives to create an environment in which it's as possible as it can be for her staff to achieve what they want to do in their parenting role, as well as be successful in the workplace. She urges young parents to incorporate events such as school commitments or participating in canteen duties into their week. She's confident they'll make up that time and reassures them that it's not going to jeopardise productivity — the same beliefs to which she remained steadfast in her own career journey.

Three quarters of her managers work around their family commitments, whether it's leaving work promptly at 5pm for their children's bedtime, or arriving late when they drop off the children. There's a *quid pro quo* on the other side, too. There will be times when Helen will expect managers to be present at an overnight retreat or participate in important strategic management meetings, in which case they need to make alternative family arrangements. She gets so much back from her staff in return — she has a high functioning team who understand how everyone works, and who trust each other. The returns to the organisation are high levels of dedication, hard work, loyalty and performance.

All HR systems are designed and technology enabled to reinforce this culture, including working from home arrangements, formal and informal recognition and reward systems, and promotion systems that recognise outcomes rather than face time in the office.

The momentum for change will accelerate, Helen believes, when more women and men with families enter senior levels, having had the experience of juggling work and home demands, and can make flexibility work for others. Leaders also have a responsibility to change the mindset of older-style managers who see women as money walking out the door when they get pregnant. She recalls meeting with a very senior politician on a field trip who was lamenting the fact that 'the problem with women is that they get pregnant'. Helen skilfully directed the discussion around how he and his workplace can maximise the return on investment in these women by creating workplaces that enable them to return and be fully productive.

Not enough women in senior positions yet? Helen advocates the introduction of targets or quotas to stop the leakage of women at the middle career level, when they are starting families. Hard targets create change. Just look at the success of women's participation in sports in the US after the introduction of Title IX, of the increase in the number of women in the police force in Victoria after Christine Nixon's initiatives, the increase in women on Boards in Australia following the introduction of targets (from 8.4 percent to 14 percent in three years), and Norway's success in mandating quotas for women on Boards (from five percent to 40 percent in seven years). In Australia the government has set targets around surpluses and growth, so why not diversity?

2. Regulatory and legal change

Secondly, Helen and other leaders have the responsibility to ensure the momentum for systemic change continues through the regulatory and legal environment that defines the conditions and entitlements of employees. It's the duty of influential leaders to fight for, and demand rights for, women. We can't expect them to fight these battles on their own, to stick their necks out without a safety net in place:

> *'The choice to have a career and a family shouldn't be up to luck or working in the public sector or having the money to buy in help. The*

> *system needs to support them. Women shouldn't have to do all the heavy lifting on their own.'*

Her roles in the union movement, as Commissioner at the Human Rights and Equal Opportunity Commission, and as the Race Discrimination Commissioner, provided her with the means to look out for women in lower paid positions, to ensure there are protections for them in enterprise agreements, or through complaints processes in Commissions that they can easily access.

3. *Societal change*

Thirdly, society needs to change. We need societies that enable women to feel comfortable about returning to the workplace as well as being a parent. Two essential components that will build the kind of society where mothers can re-enter the workforce after having children are sensible and supportive public policy around better and affordable childcare, and eliminating the tax disincentives for women wishing to return to work.

Conclusion

Helen has four key pieces of advice for women:

1. *Know what you want.* Mothers who choose to stay home are to be applauded just as much as mothers who elect to return to work. You need to decide which path is right for you.
2. *Don't line up the ducks before you start a family.* If you want to have children, don't let the moment pass you by; do it and then make it work. Take the risk, because it gets more difficult the older you are. If you decide not to have children, that's fine too.
3. *Be clear about what you want to achieve, but be flexible.* Have an open mind when it comes to opportunities that you may not have considered.
4. *Ideally, choose a workplace that understands the need for flexibility.* It should be one that rewards outcomes and productivity, rather

> than face time in the office. If you are in the unfortunate position of working in an inflexible workplace, be aware of your rights and protections.

Coming from a mother who has experienced parenting from as many angles as possible — as a single mother, stepmother, married mother, divorced mother — this sounds like well-grounded advice.

Dr Marguerite Evans-Galea

The Game of Snakes and Ladders

Dr Marguerite Evans-Galea leads international collaborations that aim to understand disease mechanism and develop novel therapies and biomarkers for repeat-associated neurodegenerative diseases. In an NHMRC-funded project, she is developing cell and gene therapies for Friedreich ataxia.

Dr Evans-Galea has received Young Investigator Awards from the Australasian Gene and Cell Therapy Society and the Friedreich Ataxia Research Alliance, US. She has also received travel awards to present her research internationally.

Committed to empowering early career researchers, Dr Evans-Galea has enjoyed supervising students and fellows in Australia and the US. She was founding Chair of the Early-Mid Career Researcher Forum with the Australian Academy of Science. She serves on the American Society for Gene and Cell Therapy Immune Responses Committee, the Australasian Gene and Cell Therapy Society Executive Committee and the Australian Science and Innovation Forum, which has partnered with the Australian Academy of Technological Sciences and Engineering. She is also a member of the Science in Australia Gender Equity Forum and co-founder of Women in Science AUSTRALIA. A strong advocate for science, Dr Evans-Galea communicates regularly via social and mainstream media. She was awarded the Australian Leadership Award in 2013.

Marguerite Evans-Galea, known to most as Maggie, is a rare breed of woman. With an insatiable curiosity, she was bitten by the mathematics and science bug from an early age, one of a small number of women electing science as a profession. Her career story runs a bit like a game of Snakes and Ladders — at some points she experienced good fortune, having been in the right place at the right time; at other times she's battled against the odds. She became pregnant, and when she excitedly told her employer, in the same conversation she was asked to 'finish up'. Eventually she found two employers who recognised her capabilities and encouraged her to realise her potential.

Becoming the mother of a beautiful baby girl was totally unexpected and changed Maggie's life forever.

Barriers to success — perpetuating myths and stereotypes

Of all the barriers that hold women back, embedded institutional mindsets and biases are probably the most insidious. One US research study on women in science, technology, engineering and mathematics (STEM)[1] identified a set of commonly held biases, assumptions and beliefs that perpetuate the dominance of men and male-centric environments in science and exclude women. In Australia, journalist and public speaker Catherine Fox[2] reflects on seven myths that dominate the Australian workplace. Both of these lists inspired me to start exploring the specific hurdles women in science must jump over.

Here is my truncated list of myths, prepared with gratitude to these two excellent publications.

Myth 1: Women can't do maths

The evidence suggests the contrary. Women have the capacity to study mathematics and science at school, and in fact Australian girls score higher in mathematics than the average for both genders compared to other OECD countries[3] (although slightly lower than

Australian boys).[4] However, this potential is being squandered as few girls choose Year 12 mathematics and science subjects. In 2004 the ratio of boys to girls studying intermediate mathematics was one girl for every 19 boys.[5] In 2004 to 2006, the percentage of girls studying combined physics and chemistry averaged 8.6 percent.[6]

This trend continues into higher education, where we are losing women at every transition point. With each step up the academic ladder, women begin to opt out. While the pipeline starts well, with almost 60 percent of Bachelor of Science graduates being women, this number drops dramatically to around 28 percent for Senior Lecturer and around ten percent for positions above that of Senior Lecturer.[7]

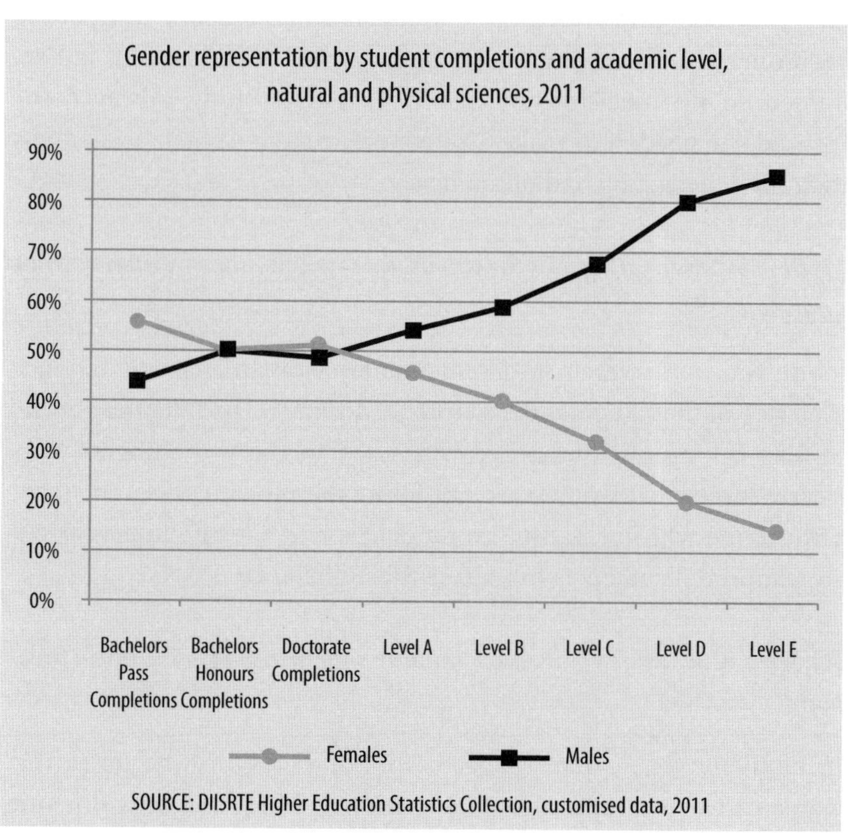

Maggie's story — smitten by science

Maggie speaks with passion about the love for learning she developed at an early age. She first visited a university at the age of 12. Coming in from regional northern Queensland to the big city, walking awestruck through the historic university was an experience that has stayed with her forever. She felt that university was where she belonged, and from then on knew she would pursue a degree. A close family friend was also very influential in this decision. He always encouraged her to work hard, study hard and get good grades.

At school Maggie was a naturally gifted musician, while she found science a challenge. She talks of the satisfaction of meeting that challenge, and this has stayed with her. So she elected to complete a rather unusual double degree — in music and science — as a path to becoming a music therapist. Having a family member with autism influenced this decision. By her third year of study, however, she realised she needed to make a career choice — music or science. By then the science bug had bitten her.

Myth 2: Women will get to the top in time, when more women become qualified

If only this myth were true. Unfortunately, women's representation at each step of the career ladder markedly declines. The statistics around women opting out of science, discussed in the preceding section, clearly shows that women are not filling the pipeline to senior roles. Time alone will not fix this conundrum, and specific interventions are required if society is to redress this imbalance.

Maggie's reflections — women missing out in the crucial mid-career point

In biomedical research, Maggie's area of expertise, she notes that women are well represented at graduate, PhD and post-doctoral fellowship levels, occupying 50 to 60 percent of positions. The next transition step to team leader or group leader is very important in a scientist's career, but often coincides with the time when many women start families, and many women leave research at this stage. In Maggie's estimate, only around 25 percent of these roles are filled by women. The pipeline becomes a mere trickle at the upper echelons of leadership, where women hold 15 percent of leadership roles.

It can be a real struggle for a woman to keep her career on track while juggling such things as having children or undertaking other carer roles. When a scientist is not physically at her desk, in the laboratory or on her computer undertaking research or producing publications, she falls behind her peers, who continue to publish, complete research and receive grants. As a scientist, publications and research grants are everything. At senior levels, women may have a team of researchers who can continue their research with limited supervision, or they are occasionally granted research funds to continue their work once they return to work or have their role replaced for a time. However, at the critical middle level this support is less likely to be available.

Myth 3: Women are not as competitive as men and don't want the top jobs

There is little evidence to support the assertion that women lack a competitive drive. Research by Bain & Company and Chief Executive Women (CEW) has consistently found that women aspire to positions of seniority at almost the same rate as men.[8]

In the science domain, similar numbers of men and women science doctorates plan to enter post-doctorate study or academic employment.[9] However, Maggie reflects that mothers face greater challenges than male scientists and women without children:

> *'Struggling to keep your track record competitive while juggling children and primary care roles, that's a real challenge. It's like elite athletes in the Olympics who have to be at the top of their game; in science you're an elite scientist for your entire career. You have to always be at the top of your game to get the funding, to get the collaborations, the international reputation.'*

Maggie's story — career interruption or career suicide?

Developing an international profile is critical for scientists, so Maggie decided to pursue her post-doctoral fellowship overseas. After talking it through with her husband Charles, also a scientist, she accepted a post-doctoral fellowship in Utah, in the mid-west of the United States. Charles became the 'trailing spouse', following Maggie's move, also entering a post-doctoral fellowship once arriving in Utah. The original plan was to be away for two years, which extended to ten.

Maggie reflects that the highest risk time to start a family is as a PhD student —you don't have much income, you don't have a track record, and you have little support, resources or influence in the workplace. It can potentially stop your career trajectory dead in the water. The risk remains high as a junior post-doctoral fellow, too; your career is just taking off, and a significant interruption can be highly detrimental without the right support in place. With children, your commitment doesn't end with maternity leave — it's for life!

Myth 4: Affirmative action programs give unfair advantages to women

This myth is an interesting one, as it assumes women take jobs away from men. This argument doesn't really hold up anywhere, and particularly not in STEM disciplines.

There are several economic reasons why inspiring more young Australian women to pursue degrees in science makes sense. Firstly, there is a supply squeeze. There is a general shortage of available STEM skills in the workforce yet the number of Year 12 students enrolling in STEM has been reducing for decades.[10]

Secondly, there is a large body of evidence that demonstrates an overwhelming business case for stimulating greater workplace diversity, including improved financial performance, leveraging talent, reflecting the customer base and marketplace, and increasing innovation.[11]

Some women relish the opportunity to participate in gender-targeted programs as a way to accelerate their career potential and to gain access to an influential network of women leaders. Maggie understands how these programs can address the specific challenges many women face and supports their implementation. However, she has never felt she had to participate in a specific 'women in science' program to accelerate her own career, and has landed scholarships on the basis of her skills and track record, rather than relying on a gender-specific affirmative action program.

Myth 5: The workplace is a meritocracy

This is the myth that the recruitment system will operate fairly to select the best candidate according to the merit of individuals.

There is a growing body of research that demonstrates that in fact our selection processes are often flawed and biased. In studies where identical résumés are assessed, men are considered more competent than women.[12] Symphony orchestras found that when they introduced blind auditions, where they assessed musicians behind a screen, suddenly they were hiring more women.[13]

If workplaces operate as a meritocracy, why do men still hold the vast majority of leadership positions in most industries? Why do many women scientists leave in the crucial career-forming years to start families, and return in such small numbers despite their ambitions to pursue a career in science?

Maggie's story — just didn't see it coming

Within the first week of starting her post-doctoral fellowship in Utah, Maggie recalls being surprised by a question she was asked by her supervisor about her plans for starting a family. 'I don't recommend it; it kills careers for women,' she recalls being told. At the time, she was shocked to hear someone express this view.

As it turned out, the comment was not too far off the mark. Looking around her team after that conversation, it was clear there were no mothers with children in her immediate workplace. There was a culture, in Utah at least, of having mothers at home, looking after children and supporting their husbands' careers. Professional ambition was expected of men, not women with children. The message was clear — she would need to choose between having a successful career and being a good mother.

Soon after commencing, Maggie experienced a health crisis that required her to take a substantial period of leave. Throughout this time she had the full support and understanding of her manager, offering her as much sick leave and flexibility as she needed. She was able to return to work, and within a couple of months received the exciting and unexpected news that she was pregnant. She went to this same supportive boss to tell him the great news. Unbelievably, he replied with: 'I think it's time for you to finish up, Maggie.' She was gobsmacked.

> *'I felt like someone had taken a cold wet fish and slapped it across my face. It was completely unexpected. But I've since seen it happen over and over again since, and so in retrospect I know my situation was not unique.'*

The next day she received a call from her supervisor, who apologised profusely. She suspects his employer had told him his comments were illegal and he should retract them. Facing such blatant discrimination during the early years of her career had been quite distressing, and Maggie's self-confidence took a hit. So she sought legal advice about her options, and decided to accept a severance package and leave the team. Perhaps if she'd had a greater sense of confidence, Maggie reflects, she would most likely have spoken up, stood her ground and negotiated more effectively.

Maggie hit the same discrimination and rejection when she started applying for other jobs. At one interview after another she realised that her pregnancy and obvious 'bump' worked against her job applications.

> *'I remember at one interview the gentleman asked me, "How do you know you'll be as good a scientist after you've had the baby?" And I*

was so inexperienced at the time that I actually sat there and tried to justify to him how I would be a good scientist, even though I'd obviously be the same person after.'

Myth 6: Women with children are more interested in family than careers

This is another myth that has little basis in fact, with research noted in Myth 3 above indicating there is little material difference in the career aspirations of men and women.

McKinsey & Company found that 79 percent of women at entry level and 83 percent of women in middle to senior levels desired to move up to the next level of work.[1]

Maggie's story — Putting family first doesn't mean putting career second

Maggie describes herself as a mother first and a scientist second, but that doesn't mean her career takes a back seat. It means, rather, that family is the anchor around which she plans her time and is her first consideration, as work can be much more easily rearranged to accommodate the needs of her family. There is no doubt she has combined the two admirably. Speaking of her relationship with her daughter Bre, she says:

> *'Everything else didn't matter. Everything else just falls away and that little person becomes the most important thing in your life. Everything I do, even to this day, is done in the context of how it is going to affect Bre; what's the impact on her.'*

Sheryl Sandberg coined the term 'leaning back' to describe the way in which many women contemplating having children consciously or unconsciously trade off their professional goals for their personal goals.[2] Maggie admits to 'leaning back' when she became pregnant. She was being pushed to apply for faculty positions and group leader roles — she had the experience and knew she was ready for it. However, she chose to stay at the same level, pursuing a second post-doctorate rather than moving up the career ladder. Perhaps it was the fear of the unknown, or perhaps not. Either way, while Maggie still feels she made the right decision for her, she believes this choice set her career back substantially, by as much as five years, not because she wasn't capable but because of the underlying biases in science; if you don't develop your career early, you are less valued. This must change, she says. 'Late bloomers' like her have so much to give to science in terms of maturity, wisdom and expertise. She feels fantastic about where her career has led her, and is confident she can make significant contributions to her area of science for another 30 or 40 years.

A white knight

Charles had accepted a position at St Jude Children's Research Hospital in Memphis (this time it was Charles's choice of job and location) and so the family relocated. Charles's supervisor casually enquired about Maggie's aspirations and career interests, and offered to help introduce her to anyone with whom she was interested in working.

She was breastfeeding at the time, not expecting to be in the market for a new job. Nevertheless, she grabbed the opportunity with both hands. This led to her interviewing with two senior investigators. They both completely understood her needs as primary carer for Bre. Like Maggie, they loved their families and loved their jobs, and understood it was no obstacle to manage both — so she accepted their offer of a post-doctoral fellowship.

These investigators gave Maggie complete flexibility around work hours, provided she met her performance outcomes and deadlines, an arrangement that enabled her to return to work full-time. She was able to pick Bre up from childcare without any sense of guilt around leaving early, or feeling she had to slink out of the office, hoping no-one would notice. Other employees were rushing for the 6pm childcare close. For Maggie, this meant she could totally focus on work during the day. In return St Jude was rewarded with higher productivity, higher engagement, greater wellbeing and reduced absenteeism, as Maggie was able to effectively maintain her work-life balance.

The work at St Jude fulfilled her intellectual desire, as well as her deeper goal of making a difference to people's lives.

> *'I could see the direct relevance. I was working with clinicians, with researchers, I was in a hospital and I was surrounded by sick children who needed help. It worked and I really developed both personally and professionally.'*

Myth 7: Women take more time off for childbearing, so are a poor investment

This myth is based around the presupposition of women being the primary carer who will stay home and look after children, and men as the main breadwinner who will remain in the workforce. Therefore, investing in women's development has a poor return on investment because they are more likely to leave the workplace.

Leading employers provide an environment that inspires women to return to work after a career break. Apart from reaping the return on investment, research shows women returning after maternity leave into flexible workplaces are the more productive, wasting only 11 percent of their day compared to other employees (men in flexible roles and all full-time employees), who waste around 14 percent of their day.[3] In an average year these women effectively deliver the equivalent of an extra week and a half of work. The bottom line is that employers in Australia and New Zealand could save at least $1.4 billion on wasted wages by employing more women on flexible arrangements.

Maggie's story — motherhood makes me a better scientist

Motherhood bestows many opportunities for learning upon someone like Maggie, probably out of necessity. For instance, her productivity has increased substantially due to her skills in organisation, ability to juggle multiple tasks and time management. Having a strict deadline in the afternoon, where the childcare operator financially penalises you if you don't pick up your child by closing time, certainly focuses the mind on getting the job done as efficiently as possible. Additionally, being a parent gives her perspective — something that comes with having multiple roles as a scientist, wife, daughter and mother. Perspective provides Maggie with the ability to step back and reflect on, rather than overreact to, criticism and to be generally happier at work. Perspective is also the cornerstone for developing resilience.

Maggie argues that women innately possess the capacity for effective teamwork, such as the ability to collaborate, mentor others and provide leadership in committees. She says that these skills are not necessarily recognised, and that we need to start looking at the whole person beyond the volume of publications they produce or grants they receive.

The ties that bind

Maggie, Charles and Bre returned to Australia in mid-2008 to be closer to their family. They also believed the Australian schooling system and lifestyle would offer more to Bre than the American one — quite frankly, the issue of gun control was one aspect about US culture that alarmed them.

Charles's career was taking off and Maggie insisted he decide the location back in Australia so he could further his career. He selected Melbourne. However, Maggie was unprepared for experiencing the reverse culture shock for the first year. Americans were so positive, she recalls, and she had forgotten how critical and cynical some Australians could be.

She now works as a research scientist at the Murdoch Childrens Research Institute at the Royal Childrens Hospital, in the 'perfect role' for her background and passions. Maggie decided to apply for grants working in gene therapy and metal ion homeostasis, in a disease known as Friedreich ataxia.[4] This work would be a natural extension of the post-doctoral work she completed in Utah and at St Jude.

She was introduced to a senior researcher who was continuing the work of a pioneer in this field. His team had received a grant and they were looking for someone with exactly Maggie's experience. It was just meant to be, she mused.

Maggie believes the Murdoch Childrens Research Institute has embraced a new way of working that maximises the potential and productivity of all its staff, including men and women who opt for flexible work practices. Being a family-friendly environment just seems to make sense when you are located within the Royal Children's Hospital, where families are front and centre of all you do. The Centre provides comprehensive information to managers and staff around planning parental leave. Managers are encouraged to commence discussions with their staff who are planning parental leave, building strategies to keep in touch over the break, participate in work where possible and ensure they are involved in key meetings if they so desire.

Maggie's current Director is the most supportive boss she has worked for to date.

> *'Martin [Maggie's Director] sees a kid from the other end of the hallway and he's there, he'll be talking to them. He'll welcome people back from maternity leave and let them know their child is welcome any time to the meetings.'*

What Maggie's story reveals — beyond the myths

Juggling two demanding roles

Maggie's story, like many others in this book, demonstrates the ongoing challenges of combining a successful professional career with personal fulfilment. 'Leaning back' in her career meant that even though the career adapted, it took more time.

She has had to deal with a mountain of mother guilt, some of which may have been self-inflicted. She remembers the first day she and Charles dropped Bre off at childcare — she sat in the car and cried. Bre didn't seem to mind, though; she had new friends to play with and new toys.

Reflecting back on that time, Maggie has some advice to share about coping with this guilt. In her experience:

- Learn to live with it. However, talking about it, sharing your feelings and supporting other women with similar feelings is very important.
- Get some perspective. Your child may not be as traumatised as you are about going to childcare.
- Importantly, there is no need to create formal experiences, go on expensive holidays or buy expensive toys. Just 'hanging out together' can be more effective.
- Communication with your child is very important. Maggie notices that if she is particularly busy, Bre can become a bit needy and want to be with her more. So she always communicates what is coming up — if it's grant season she'll explain that 'Mum will be very busy' and will explain the deadline, after which they will do something special together.
- Every six weeks Maggie and Bre have a mother-daughter day. This gives Bre some certainty that Mum will be there for her, and it's something to look forward to.
- Don't be afraid to ask for help. Accepting that you'll need a hand every now and then will make you feel more in control — it is all part of the process.

Tackling the practicalities of parenting

Agreeing on the division of housework and childcare responsibilities creates a sense of being in control, a partnership and shared experience. While Charles and Maggie shared all household and childcare tasks equally, including changing nappies, when it came to needing to leave work early for appointments and activities, they agreed it would be less disruptive to their careers if one parent took on that responsibility. Maggie took on this role.

Someone to watch over me

Mentors and advocates are invaluable to women, especially early on in their careers; many successful women credit mentorship with helping them build their careers. However, mentors may be scarce in unbalanced occupations or industries, such as those based around STEM capabilities. Maggie advocates seeking a mentor outside your organisation to help give perspective, challenge your thinking and provide alternative approaches you may not have considered.

Imposter syndrome

Early in Maggie's career she was plagued by self-doubt, or what she recognised as the 'imposter syndrome': feeling she was a fraud, underestimating her contribution, and believing that she didn't deserve the position she'd been given

Maggie's experiences have taught her that the imposter syndrome is easily triggered by her self-critical internal voice, which can end up becoming a self-fulfilling prophecy. She has also learned that while it is hard to shake these feelings, once you recognise and name them you can effectively challenge your internal critic and learn to believe in your own abilities. This is the start of shifting from the mindset of 'I'm not ready' to 'I want to put my hand up for this'.

The right employer is the key

Find the right employer and the right manager, and your professional ambitions can be realised. *Sideways To The Top* provides an organisation checklist, which offers a due diligence framework for assessing your future employer.[5]

Ultimately, workplaces where part-time or flexible work and career breaks are not considered a career killer and are routinely accessed by women *and* men, where leaders understand the productivity and innovation spin-offs that diversity brings, is becoming the new normal. Women and men shouldn't stand for anything less. Heather Carmody in *Sideways To The Top* sums it up well when she says:

> *'A lack of diversity is a race to extinction. If you can't attract, develop and promote women, you know you're losing ground in the labour market and workplace culture. If a bunch of lookalike blokes is the best you can do and the best you want to do, you can be certain you will have a problem. Those blokes are a shrinking pool. The growth is with non-lookalike blokes … and women.'*[6]

Anna Burke and Kelly O'Dwyer

Parenthood and Politics — Then and Now

Anna Burke has served as the elected representative for Chisholm since the 1998 Federal Election and served as Speaker of the House of Representatives in the 43rd Parliament.

As an active and approachable local Member of Parliament, Anna is well known throughout Chisholm and committed to assisting members of her local community. Many Australians from across the country know Anna not only for her role in the Speaker's Chair, but for her highly successful campaign to protect people from unwanted telemarketing calls. In 2005, Anna moved a Private Member's Bill in Federal Parliament to create a national 'Do Not Call' list, which pressured the former government into adopting her policy.

Anna has a Bachelor of Arts (Honours) Degree from Monash University and a Master of Commerce (Honours) from the University of Melbourne.

Prior to entering Federal Parliament, Anna worked as a national industrial officer for the Finance Sector Union, where she represented the workers in the banking, finance and insurance industries. Anna has also worked in human relations for VicRoads, and for the Victorian Institute of Technology (now Victoria University).

Anna lives in Box Hill South with her husband Steve and their two children.

Kelly O'Dwyer was elected to Federal Parliament in a by-election in December 2009 at the age of 32 to represent her local electorate of Higgins. On 23 December 2014 she was sworn in as the Parliamentary Secretary to the Treasurer. Kelly was a member of the House of Representatives Standing Committee on Economics from 2010, serving as Chairman from 2013.

Kelly is the founder and Chairman of the Parliamentary Friends of Women in Science, Maths and Engineering, and serves as an Ovarian Cancer Ambassador, Patron of the Stonnington City Brass and of the East Malvern Junior Girls Football Team.

Kelly graduated from the University of Melbourne with Honours in Law and an Arts Degree. Upon leaving university, she embarked on a legal career at Freehills, practicing in corporate law.

In 2004, Kelly commenced as an economic policy advisor to the former Federal Treasurer, the Hon. Peter Costello AC, responsible for several key policy areas including competition law and competition policy, foreign investment and private equity. In 2007, Kelly undertook a new role as an executive at National Australia Bank, where she was involved in building a new business area.

Kelly is a former board member of Bowls Australia and was also member of the Victorian Advisory Council of Camp Quality, an organisation supporting children and families affected by cancer.

Meet the honourable Anna Burke and Kelly O'Dwyer, MPs for their Victorian constituencies of Chisholm and Higgins respectively. There is a great contrast between these women's backgrounds, family life and political persuasions, but their interests and values align in at least one area — they're both passionate about increasing opportunities and choices for women who start families and who also want a successful working life. Now they have one more thing in common: in May 2015, when Kelly embarked on parenthood for the first time, they are now both mothers in the Australian parliament.

Here are their stories. Anna, a working-class, street-smart Labor Party politician, was in 1999 only the second female member of the House of Representatives to have a child while in office. Kelly, a younger but no less successful Liberal Party politician, holds the plum seat of Higgins in the leafy inner-east of Melbourne, and will be only the third woman on the Liberal side of politics to have a baby while in parliament, is the first ever female Parliamentary Secretary to the Treasurer, and the first woman member for her seat of Higgins. She'll be in good company. A cohort comprising nine women Members of Parliament have had a child while in office since Anna,[1] and two other women, Kate Ellis and Amanda Rishworth, have given birth earlier this year.

Both women were prepared to share their experiences and expectations of juggling their roles as mother and politician. Some of the fascinating questions we explored included: Why go into politics? How will their experiences of parenthood differ? Can the intense pace and ruthless culture of parliament accommodate the specific needs of families? Has parliament broken the code around designing a workplace where women who are mothers can participate?

Anna Burke's story — the way it was

'I never wanted to be a Member of Parliament.'

The middle daughter of five children, Anna grew up amid a large, hard-working extended family. Her father was one of ten children, her mother one of three. Both parents instilled an ethic of hard work in their children. Her mother was a teacher who later upgraded her qualifications to become a teacher/librarian, her father earned a low wage as a bank worker, and neither had been able to afford to go to university. They insisted, however, that all their children get the best education possible. After attending a Catholic school, Anna was off to Monash University following the abolition of university fees during the Whitlam era.

Anna's parents were not political, but the family was far from sheltered from world affairs. They ensured their children understood their place in the world, raising them to be conscious of the social justice issues confronting the needy. Current affairs also played a big part in their lives. They watched the news every evening, debated the facts and developed in their children a sense of social justice. The area of Ashwood had a very strong local community focus, and Anna's family were heavily involved in the school and the church. Anna recalls, 'My mother was on every committee going. You helped others, you looked out for others.'

She was brought up to understand that nothing is given to you — you have to work for it. Although her parents were regular battlers, she never felt deprived. However, she remembers one Christmas where she just couldn't work out Santa's motivations.

'Why does Santa give more presents to the kids across the road than to us?' she asked her mother, trying to work out the justice of the situation.

'Oh well, you know, Santa has to spread it around,' answered her mother, trying in vain to come up with an explanation.

Anna joined the local branch of the Labor Party because she wanted to influence change: 'I can sit back and complain or I can get involved. You can chuck rocks from the sidelines or you can be in the middle of it.'

Not a cushy professional career or role in a politician's office for Anna. She brought her life experience in a tough blokey world with her during her somewhat unexpected move into politics. Her first role at VicRoads was compulsorily acquiring homes for roadworks ('You think being a politician is hard? How about: "I'm taking your house. I'm bulldozing it and putting up a road."'). She then worked in Industrial Relations at Victoria University during its transition into a university ('It was trauma and I lasted 12 months.'). She finally shifted onto the employee side of the fence when she became an Industrial Officer with the Finance Sector Union after the amalgamation of two unions ('It didn't get easier!').

In 1997 she was pre-selected by the Labor Party to contest the seat of Chisholm, a safe Liberal seat recently vacated by well-respected Liberal Party member Dr Michael Wooldridge. She reluctantly stood, and few in the Labor Party expected her to win, thinking there was no way she would wrest a safe seat from the Liberals, especially the first time around. Anna felt the same way and assured her husband, 'It's alright, I can't win.'

She campaigned well ('I never do anything by halves.'), winning over the battlers with her no-frills style, fitting in, being an approachable person, and comfortable campaigning in her local area, which she knew like the back of her hand. Towards the end of the campaign it began to dawn on her that she might win. So she rang up a friend and asked, 'Look, what does a Member of Parliament do?'

'A big white car will come for you, Anna, and you'll go to Canberra,' she replied.

'Okay, I can do that. And I'm going to get paid more. Sounds good.'

Not that it was an easy ride for her. There was one frightening time during the campaign when a postcard was circulated in her electorate with the message, 'Wish you were here', pointing to her house and including her current address in Newport (they had recently moved to Newport for her husband Stephen's job; Anna had committed to returning to her home electorate should she win). At that stage Stephen was working shifts and Anna was home alone at nights, feeling vulnerable and frightened. She wondered if they would have done this to a bloke.

Anna had her first child, Madeleine (Maddie) in 1998, 12 months after being elected. She came up against the typical stereotyping and awkwardness many men express when she told them of her pregnancy. The leader of the Party, she says, didn't have a clue, didn't know what to do. Others asked her questions, such as: 'Will you take time off?' 'Will you come back?' 'How are you going to cope?' 'How is Steve going to cope?'

'Of course I'll take time off, of course I'll come back, we'll manage,' she retorted. 'Have you got a problem with any of the blokes and their partners? Why isn't it an issue for them?' She is still frustrated that women politicians become defined by their motherhood status; she remembers Jackie Kelly being constantly referred to as 'the pregnant Jackie Kelly'. She doubts they would ever describe a man in terms of his status as an expectant father.

Anna returned to Canberra with a brand new four-week-old baby. 'It was insane, but nobody knew what to do,' she recalls. Stephen applied for part-time work and was knocked back — part-time work was for mothers, not fathers, he was told. He fought and eventually won the right to take 12 months leave without pay and then to return to work part-time. Anna remembers those 12 months as a blur. Some days parliament didn't finish sitting until 11pm, and feeding times didn't coincide with sitting times. Yet Maddie was not really a problem — 'Young babies are quite portable,' Anna reflects.

As a parliamentarian she believes she has more flexibility than in other workplaces, especially back in her home electorate. Maddie would often come into the office at Chisholm, she would play or sleep in the cot, and Anna would feed her around meetings. But you can't plan for every eventuality. Anna recalls one day in Canberra, with Stephen having gone for a swim at a time when Anna thought there would be no business in the House. Suddenly, the Division bells were ringing, Anna's staff member wasn't there and she was left literally 'holding the baby'. There was nothing for it but to take the baby into the House:

> *'So the Speaker sends me a note saying, "Anna, I haven't drawn*

> *attention to it but there is a stranger in the house," because only parliamentarians are allowed to sit in the green chairs. So I sent one back saying, "I don't think Maddie's about to bring down democracy, but I take your point."'*

The next time this happened Anna was better prepared — she went into the Whip's office and handed her baby over to one of the staff there to look after her. Many of the staffers loved having a baby in parliament; it normalised an otherwise sterile workplace.

There's a first time for everything. Anna says the workplace wasn't accommodating for children at first. Dealing with the trappings of a baby, such as a baby capsule in the Comcar, a cot in her office, a high chair and a change table, were not prescribed in any policy manual, so each event needed to be worked through. Other difficulties included trying to find accommodation in Canberra that would suit a baby, and bringing an extra set of clothes for dealing with a baby being sick on them on the way to a meeting. They also had to plan Stephen's trips to Canberra carefully, as partners were given a fixed number of airfares a year.

By the time baby John came along two years later, the workplace operated like clockwork in comparison to those early days. She was able to take three months leave from parliament and by then several other women politicians also had babies, so she was not so much of an oddity. She was fortunate her sister-in-law was available for support in Melbourne and could also travel with her to Canberra, while Stephen looked after Maddie in Melbourne. Besides, John was an easy-going baby, despite needing a lot of medical attention during his first 12 months.

Parenting two children was a whole new experience. Anna and Stephen were juggling childcare, driving them both to school, volunteering for tuck shop hours, attending parent teacher nights and doctor's appointments, caring for them when they were sick, the rounds of surgery, attending school plays, and various weekend commitments. Sadly, during this time both Anna's mother-in-law and grandmother passed away.

Juggling it all doesn't mean doing it all, but it does mean organising your domestic life and being innovative. Anna says she learnt organisational skills from her mother, who studied, looked after five children and managed the household. Anna's organisation is legendary — such as her famous freezer, in which she stores prepared frozen meals for the week, all labelled with instructions. Or having a cupboard full of presents for those times when a children's birthday party unexpectedly comes up. At the start of the year her days in Canberra would be posted on the fridge, so everyone knew when she'd be gone.

Saturday morning bake-offs, fortnightly Sunday family dinners with the extended family of 23 aunts, uncles and cousins, special days with Mum — these formed an integral part of the ebb and flow of their lives. My personal favourite anecdote was how Anna would read Maddie and John bedtime stories through Skype. I can just see them tucked up in bed, with the computer in front of them and Anna holding up the book at the other end, saying, 'Here's the picture.'

Both children were accustomed to Anna's routine and her absences, provided they knew what was happening. The difficulties were the unexpected periods of time in Canberra, or the weekend commitments, when Maddie and John wanted her to be home for them. Taking on the role of Speaker of the House created such tensions, with significant overseas travel, longer hours and extended days in Canberra.

What struck me about Anna's skill in combining her work and family commitments was that her children were part and parcel of her life, not an add-on. Visit her office back then and you'd come across them playing in the corner, participating in Clean Up Australia, or attending local celebrations.

Conflicts between her responsibilities as mother and politician were generally managed, except for one time when Maddie's first day of school clashed with a leadership challenge in the Labor Party — Kim Beazley was challenging Rudd (yes, men do it too, not just red-headed women). For Anna to cast her vote, she needed to be physically in Canberra. Here's what happened:

> *'So Kim Beazley rings me: "Anna, I'd like your vote." "Kim, I'd love to vote for you but I'm not going to be there. I'm going to take Maddie to her first day of school." Kevin Rudd rang me, I said, "Kevin, I'll be honest. I was going to give my vote to Kim, but it doesn't matter, I'm not coming." Both of them said fine, they understand. Lots of my colleagues rang and said, "Anna, you are mad. You have to be there. This will be counted against you." Even my mother rang and said, "You've got to think about this." I said, "I have. And I only have one option and that is I am taking Maddie to school." "She won't remember," they said. "I don't care, I will remember. This is an important step. I'm going to be there and if it counts against me, well, so what? She's going to be here forever, my career in parliament's not."'*

Having children early on in a parliamentary career is easier, Anna believes, than bringing young children with you who are not used to the bizarre routines of Canberra life. If children have been born into, and brought up with, the 20-week Canberra regime and everything that comes with being a Federal politician, they go with the flow, whereas an enormous adjustment is required by children, particularly around the travel and absences, especially if someone moves into politics from a previously stable job.

Anna would advise women politicians having children to plan everything, and let everyone in the family know these plans, but don't stress if the plans go awry. Forgive yourself when things don't work out, like when you've forgotten to organise a child pick-up or buy a present for one of your children's friend's birthday party. Have a backup plan, such as friends who you reciprocate with, and other family members in emergencies. Secondly, stay fit. You'll need all your energy and resources for those sleep-deprived days, weeks or months. Thirdly, don't be dictated by what others think. Set boundaries for yourself and learn to say no. You must do what is right for your family and your circumstances, not what others expect.

Kelly O'Dwyer's story — the way it is today

Kelly's journey has been different to Anna's. Her political awakening followed a visit by Lorraine Elliott, the newly minted member for Mooroolbark, to her school. From that time on she started to think big. She wanted to be part of something beyond her own world, where she could really make a difference: 'I remember thinking at the time that she [Lorraine Elliott] was doing a job that had real value and real meaning.'

Yet the seeds were sown much earlier than this encounter. Kelly was raised to have a very strong sense of responsibility. The eldest of four children, she comes from a close family. She has always had an enquiring mind, and big issues of the day were frequently discussed around the O'Dwyer dinner table. While neither of her parents were politically active, she was taught values around the importance of family, reward for effort, taking personal responsibility, and valuing freedom of choice. This led her to consider how she could make her own contribution to the economic prosperity of her community: 'One of the greatest gifts my mother has ever given me is the conviction that you can do anything if you put your mind to it, you're committed to it and you work hard.'

From their example of being active in the local community, her parents instilled in her a belief that making the most of her education was an obligation and contributing to her community was part of her personal responsibility.

After graduating from the University of Melbourne with a combined Arts/Law Degree, she commenced her legal career in corporate law at Herbert Smith Freehills, a top-tier law firm in Melbourne. In 2004 she became Economic Policy Advisor, then Senior Advisor to the Federal Treasurer. Three years later she accepted a senior executive role at the National Australia Bank. In December 2009, at the age of 32, she was elected in a by-election to represent the seat of Higgins, following the resignation of the Treasurer.

Being able to make a successful contribution to politics and simultaneously a successful family life was a non-negotiable for Kelly. She fully respects women who decide otherwise, who decide to be a stay-at-home mum. After all, this is the choice her own mother made, and Kelly understands that she is the beneficiary of that choice. People need to make the right choice for their family and for their circumstances. Having freedom of choice is the important element, and an issue for which Kelly is prepared to fight (but more of that later).

Despite her convictions that she could manage both a parliamentary career and have a successful family life, there were not many female role models in parliament. This weighed on Kelly's mind. She consulted extensively with her husband, Jon, and her extended family before finally deciding to enter politics. 'I did think about that very deeply before putting up my hand for parliament. But once I'd got my head around that I must say I thought, *I think it's completely doable*.'

Unlike many other women politicians, who were pre-selected for marginal seats, Kelly was pre-selected to the strong seat of Higgins, held by two former prime ministers and a former Treasurer. Nevertheless, her gender was still an issue among some conservative decision-makers, who asked her several questions during pre-selection that they would never have asked men, about her personal life and intentions to start a family. Kelly recalls being 'fascinated and rather horrified' by the experience of a friend of hers going through the same pre-selection process many years ago, who was asked about the impact children would have on her ability to fulfil her role. The question was clearly loaded, with the implication that she couldn't be both a good mother *and* a successful politician. Kelly hastens to add that it was a many years ago and she believes these attitudes have shifted. Increasing the number of women in parliament is an important and obvious step towards improved and representative decision-making, says Kelly, as women parliamentarians can bring different life experiences and perspectives to debates and discussions that their women constituents hold.

Treasurer Joe Hockey was hugely supportive of Kelly when she advised him of her pregnancy. Joe had himself taken three months leave after the birth of his first child. He and his wife, Melissa Babbage, head of Global Finance at Deutche Bank, juggle careers and three children.

The timing of her impending confinement is a little unfortunate. Kelly, having been appointed Parliamentary Secretary to the Treasurer, knows the next budget is due to be released in May — about the time the baby is due. Joe Hockey has worked with her to recalibrate workloads and responsibilities to ensure the transition is as seamless as possible.

Kelly plans to take around two months maternity leave after the birth of her baby, and will work from her home office. Her husband plans to take around five months parental leave to support her, and will travel to Canberra with her and the baby. Having a highly capable and supportive team in her local office that can efficiently prioritise work is a great bonus. Beyond that, Kelly has her family as backup when needed.

She considers herself fortunate in her family circumstances to have choices around staying home or returning to work, unlike many families where two incomes are essential and the second income-earner (usually the woman) feels compelled to return to work.

Kelly is exasperated by some of the existing structures and policies that limit freedom of choice for women when it comes to re-entering the workforce. She says it results in a lower labour force participation rate for Australian women compared to other OECD countries. Like all parents, she wants the best for her children — she wants them to be well cared for in a safe and nurturing environment. Families should have options beyond the mother having to quit her job to provide this environment.

Two of the biggest impediments to women returning to the workforce are childcare and the taxation system. The current restrictive, high-cost childcare options need to be expanded to meet the differing needs and budgets of families. The current tax and transfer system needs to change so mothers are not financially disadvantaged by re-entering the workforce.[2]

Resolving these issues and enabling more women to return to work makes good business and economic sense, says Kelly. Employers who provide flexible workplaces where women can return to work retain excellent employees in whom they have invested. Additionally, they will help lift aggregate productivity and economic prosperity, and will reduce reliance on the pension system.

Why are women still under-represented in parliament?

Things have changed since Anna first began working in parliament. A childcare centre has been built for parents with children at Parliament House, voting by proxy or email has been introduced, and women politicians with families are starting to be the norm. The hours have also been less extreme since Dr Mal Washer convinced John Howard in 2010 to restrict late-night sitting times for occupational health and safety reasons.[3]

However, women continue to be significantly under-represented in Australian parliament and executive government, comprising less than 1/3 of all parliamentarians and 1/5 of all ministers. In 2014 the World Bank ranked Australia a dismal 48th in the world for representation of women in national parliaments, down from 20th position in 2001.[4]

There are a range of structural, cultural and social factors that inhibit women's political participation, some of which have been discussed above, including pre-selection practices, the challenges women face in balancing work and family responsibilities, and discriminatory views about women in politics. What about the adversarial nature of the parliamentary environment? Parliament can be a hectic, bizarre and tough place, demanding long hours and total dedication. If Question Time is anything to go by, it's not a family-friendly environment. Norman Abjorensen, ABC journalist, describes Australian politics as:

> *'a rough and tumble hurly burly of Hobbesian war of all against all; an endless scramble up the greasy pole of power and down again;*

> *an eternal battle in which there are few winners but many losers ... Every player is ambitious; loyalties are elastic and situational; ruthlessness knows no bounds; hatreds are many and unrelenting. Very few, if any, of those who attain power do so with clean hands.*'[5]

Has this aggressive 'anything goes' culture recently been taken to a new low? Many would think so. Paul Keating, former Labor Treasurer, was famous for his scathing character assassinations, calling former prime minister John Howard 'a dead carcass swinging in the breeze', and Andrew Peacock a 'painted, perfumed gigolo' and an 'intellectual rust bucket'.[6] Compare this with the sexist and misogynistic comments thrown at former prime minister Julia Gillard when she was in office, which seem to take these insults to a new low — Bill Heffernan described her as having 'chosen to remain deliberately barren', placards with the words 'Ditch the Witch' and 'Bob Brown's bitch' painted on them, and Alan Jones' comment that her father had 'died of shame'. These insults and jibes filled Julia Gillard with rage, culminating in her famed misogyny speech in parliament in 2012 that went viral on social media.[7] Her experience with sexism demonstrates how challenging it still is for women to succeed in politics.

The issue of gender diversity is currently being recognised and addressed by both major parties. Caroline Elliott is the Vice President of the Victorian Division of the Liberal Party, and drove the recent report that was handed down at the Victorian State Council. The report calls for greater diversity in pre-selection and the need to address gender discrimination in the Liberal Party. Caroline conducted this review in conjunction with the Hon. Kay Patterson, former Health Minister. The newly elected President of the Liberal Party, Michael Kroger, has vowed to address the gender discrimination issues identified in this report. The Labor Party has had targets in place for several years, and recently confirmed a target of 40 percent of all winnable Labor seats to be held by women. Time will tell whether these commitments will finally overcome this long-standing and seemingly intractable problem.

Yet the bigger challenge for a democracy is how to bring different views and life experience into discussions, debates and decision-making beyond just the gender perspective. For parliament to be truly representative it should reflect and engage with the social diversity of the Australian population, including perspectives of different cultural, religious, social, sexual and age groups. How can a Cabinet primarily comprising white, middle-class, middle-aged, educated Catholic men (and two women), with backgrounds in law or as parliamentary staffers, do anything else but create a monoculture that mirrors their own life's experiences and values and be in furious agreement with each other around their views and ideals? It seems the prevailing status quo must irrevocably alter for our democratic system to become truly representative.

Where to from here?

In one way, this chapter finishes mid-story. Kelly and her husband have only just welcomed their first child into their lives, and her experiences with negotiating the clashes of a politician's life and motherhood will be just starting. However, these days she won't be alone in parliament.

Perhaps Anna Bligh, former Queensland Premier, sums it up best at the end of her biography, *Through the Wall*, when she concludes:

> *'There is only one thing that will diminish and eliminate all the constituent parts of the wall and that's a constant stream of other women pushing through it until it crumbles altogether. As we work for a more balanced sharing of power, in our parliaments, in our workplaces and in our lives, we are busting up the status quo … as women shift into leadership roles in all spheres of life, the novelty will begin to wear off, the isolating sense of difference will dissipate, the experience will be normalised and opponents will be silenced.'*[8]

Anna Burke and other mothers in parliament have fought the battles to have motherhood recognised and accepted as an intrinsic part of parliamentary life, and have begun to break down the obstacles facing women who want to be both an effective politician and a successful mother. Kelly's experience as a new mum is beginning to become the norm in parliament, and hopefully she will experience greater acceptance from any remaining opponents.

Stop the press!

Just before going to print I met Kelly again, three weeks after giving birth to a beautiful baby girl, Olivia. Kelly was back on her first official engagement, welcoming the prime minister's announcement of a $4 million grant to Very Special Kids to purchase their purpose-built palliative care facility in Malvern. Work doesn't go on hold when you're a Member of Parliament. Jon was taking care of Olivia in the meantime. They are both totally in love with her, she says.

It's back to Canberra in a few weeks, returning to the heated debates and controversial political issues of the day, the budget being the major one. Jon will be on hand in Canberra to provide the support she needs. She recognises there will be much to learn about juggling motherhood, travel and her responsibilities as Member for Higgins and Parliamentary Secretary to the Treasurer. She will be in good company, with the Hon. Kate Ellis having given birth to a baby boy in April, and the Hon. Amanda Rishworth a boy in March. Quite a striking threesome of support. Sounds like it's fasten your seatbelts (or is that the baby capsule?) for a fast ride!

Lucinda Nolan

A Force to be Reckoned With

Lucinda Nolan is the Deputy Commissioner of Regional Operations, responsible for all regional frontline services as well as specialist capabilities within the State Emergencies & Security Command, Transit & Public Safety Command and the new Family Violence Command. In this role, Lucinda's focus is on reforming and improving the effectiveness of police service delivery.

Prior to this, she was the Deputy Commissioner, Strategy, a role in which she oversaw Professional Standards, Media and Corporate Communications, People Development, Corporate Strategy and Operational Improvement, and Service Delivery Reform Group. Her focus was on developing and implementing reforms to ensure that Victoria Police was efficient, effective and flexible in tackling changing emerging issues and risks.

She has been a member of Victoria Police since 1983, and has a broad and diverse background, encompassing frontline policing, criminal investigations and taskforce work, internal investigations, strategy and planning, education, intelligence management, and media and corporate communications. She also has extensive experience in major event management, large scale criminal investigations and counter terrorism.

Lucinda has been awarded a Bachelor of Arts (Honours) and Master of Arts (both from the University of Melbourne), as well as a Graduate Diploma in Public Sector Management. She has also recently successfully completed the Advanced Management Program at Harvard University. In 2011, Lucinda was awarded the Australian Police Medal for distinguished service to policing.

Interviewing Lucinda Nolan, it became obvious that a one-hour conversation was barely enough to scratch the surface of the extent of her policing career. Her 32 years in policing since graduating from the Police Academy in 1983 ranged far and wide, before she scaled the heights to Deputy Police Commissioner. Perhaps this breadth, coupled with her pragmatic approach, is why she has garnered so much respect among the rank and file of the police force. She has succeeded in the midst of a tough police culture, challenged the seamy underbelly of Melbourne, and understands policing from the ground up. Yet she retains a relatively low public profile. This made the interview all the more intriguing.

Sisters are doing it for themselves — women in policing

Lucinda's story is, in many ways, a natural evolution of the story of women in policing. This story began in 1917, with the appointment of the first two policewomen in New South Wales, Madge O'Connor and Elizabeth Beers (Victoria followed in 1923). These women were pioneers — they were gutsy, forthright, vocal activists for equal rights, equal recognition and equal pay. Policewomen won the right for equal pay relatively early, in 1924, however equal recognition for their work was a long way off. They were prohibited from wearing uniforms and their role was restricted to the welfare of women and children: 'to protect women and girls from being molested, prevent truancy, examine women in cases of sexual offence, and supervise thoughtless girls and young soldiers'.

It took almost 30 years for the first woman to be appointed to the lowest non-commissioned rank — Katherine McKay, promoted to Senior Constable in 1943. Shortly thereafter they designed their own uniform, though it was without epaulettes as they were told they would never make officer. It wasn't until the 1980s that women were appointed to the positions of Superintendent and Assistant Commissioner. The first woman Police Commissioner, Christine Nixon, was appointed in 2001. Today, women in senior ranks of the police force are less of a novelty, with 38 female Inspectors, four female Superintendents, three female Assistant Commissioners and one Deputy Commissioner.[1]

The start of the journey

Unlike many police officers, Lucinda had not been born into a police family or bred to be a police officer. Her father started work as a very young boy with the Postmaster General's Office, now Telstra, for his entire working life. Lucinda's parents understood the value of a good education and, despite financial hardship, scraped together enough money to put their children through private Catholic schools. Lucinda and her three siblings were therefore brought up with a good dose of down-to-earth middle-class values, coupled with a private school education.

After completing a Bachelor of Psychology with Honours from the University of Melbourne in 1982, Lucinda had planned to become a clinical psychologist. However, her brother suggested she gain some 'real life experience' for a year or two in the police force before completing her Masters. This gap year led to a lifelong commitment to policing; she was hooked from day one. Policing was a natural fit with Lucinda's high energy levels and strong work ethic, and she loved the diversity her career in law enforcement offered. No two days are ever the same, she muses, and her entire workday can change instantly. Later in her career, she found she was able to apply the disciplined research, analytical and conceptual skills her university studies had nurtured all those years before, demonstrating that no career-based experience is wasted.

Right place and time

The 1980s was a decade in which opportunities for women were opening up in the police force, and a small number of women were rising to positions of prominence. Lucinda was one of four women in her squad when she graduated from the Victorian Police Academy in 1983, but she almost didn't make it. In 1986, when promoted to detective, she took a phone call from a man who had been on the original selection panel. He congratulated her on her promotion, saying he had always kept a watching brief on her career. She was astonished to hear the selection panel would have rejected her application if he hadn't intervened only because they felt they'd selected enough women for the intake that year. Yet he had seen something in her, and convinced the panel to make an exception to let one more woman through. Without this intervention, Lucinda would have walked away devastated. She knew she had passed the rigorous physical training and the written examinations, so would have concluded she must have had some personality flaw that excluded her. An unspoken gender quota system would have been the last thing on her mind.

Lucinda was thrown into the realities of fighting crime from her first day. Her initial postings covered some of the toughest police precincts in Melbourne, including West Melbourne and Prahran, before she moved on to hard-edged detective work. These postings were followed by time in the Rape Squad, working with the Spectrum Taskforce investigating the notorious Mr Cruel abductions, and afterwards a stint in Security and Intelligence. She rounded out her experience with a range of head office roles in Professional Standards, Policy and Planning, and Media and Corporate Communications, before her appointment to Assistant Commissioner, then Deputy Commissioner.

The early years were marked by a spate of police shootings and citizen attacks, among them the 'Mad Max' Marinoff killings in 1985, the Russell Street police headquarters bombing in 1986 in which police constable Angela Taylor was killed, the Queen Street and Hoddle Street massacres in 1987, and the Walsh Street police shootings in 1988, when two of Lucinda's colleagues were brutally murdered. She was in Sydney with the police netball team at the time they heard the news — a hideous time, she recalls, which she hopes she never has to relive.

In the 1980s, the emotional and psychological distress for police officers experiencing traumatic events was severely underestimated. There were no trauma support groups, clinical counselling or therapy available. Police officers were just expected to deal with it in their own way. This was when the camaraderie, mateship and teamwork for which the police force is known was so crucial — being able to grieve together and discuss their emotions created support in times of need.

Navigating the police culture

In her biography, Christine Nixon describes the poisonous culture war within police ranks. She identifies what she terms the 'closed, cloistered, fractured cult of policing', describing aspects of the police culture as 'the exclusive brethren of blokes, entrenched in rituals of bad behaviour that ostracises so many good men, as well as most women'.[2] In her experience, women still have a long way to go in police ranks, as evidenced in the scarcity of women alongside her in senior ranks.

Times have changed somewhat since Christine Nixon's words, says Lucinda, although she acknowledges that hardcore elements of the police force still persist, especially in those traditional operational areas that perhaps are the last fortresses of male dominance.

The most significant challenge for men and women wishing to combine a successful career in policing with family responsibilities lies not necessarily with antiquated attitudes about the role of women in the police force, Lucinda believes, but in the unpredictable nature of police work. This aspect makes it virtually impossible to plan longer-term childcare arrangements with any degree of certainty. The demand on police can change daily, driven by operational demands, such as responding to unplanned protest activity or industrial disputes, making it very difficult to predict working days. This uncertainty streams many women with children out of operational roles and into administrative or office-based roles with standard hours, in order to manage the work/family conundrum. There came a time in Lucinda's career when she had to face this conundrum head-on.

Rolling with the punches

Lucinda and her husband Paul, also a police officer, decided to start a family soon after they got married. She fell pregnant with their first son when she was a detective in the Mr Cruel investigation (Mr Cruel was an Australian murderer and rapist in Melbourne during the late 1980s and early 1990s). After returning from 12 months maternity leave, she was offered a plum job in the Violent Crime Analysis Unit, commencing with overseas training with world-class criminal profiling experts. She was very excited about the opportunity and accepted the offer, but at the last minute the role fell through. She decided this could be an opportune time to grow her family, so within three years the couple had two more children, another boy and a girl.

Then the unexpected happened — their oldest son Liam was diagnosed with autism at about 18 months old. Lucinda and Paul had to make some key decisions about their careers. As Lucinda recalls:

> *'I've had three kids and my eldest has a disability, so I knew that it was either resign or work. We knew in terms of finances that I couldn't resign because we were going to need the money for occupational therapists, speech pathologists, psychologists and other medical expenses. So my husband and I made the decision then and there that we were just going to have to work our way through it as best we could.'*

Lucinda decided to step back from detective work, taking on a range of administrative roles for several years. In later years Paul did the same, transferring to an office job. In this way they both ensured they were able to be part of their children's school and personal lives, attending sporting events, speech nights, participating on the school council and in working bees. Lucinda was fortunate to work for managers who recognised her ability and were prepared to offer her the flexibility she needed to accommodate family arrangements. They allowed her to work long shifts to accumulate hours, using time in lieu to attend medical appointments for Liam or meet important school commitments. In return, Lucinda gave back in spades, fully committed to ensuring she delivered quality outcomes on time and without compromise. The flexibility the workplace provided enabled her to continue to work at a senior level, undertaking significant work and remaining visible so that when the time came to get back on the promotion track she was ready.

However, these were tremendously tough years. They just scraped by after the nanny and the medical bills had been paid. Lucinda and Paul barely saw each other, working opposite shifts so at least one of them was present for the children in the early days. Raising a child with autism is a constant challenge, requiring 24/7 commitment. There was no time for personal indulgences, such as reading or regular exercise. Having an autistic child meant that day trips or visits to unfamiliar places were too stressful. There could be no extended family holidays.

No-one can care constantly without a break, however. This was where support from the couple's parents was critical; they looked after the children during emergencies and for scheduled weekends away so Lucinda and Paul could spend time together.

The children were also a great support to each other. They were always highly supportive of Liam, and from a very young age were discerning about their friendship groups. Even as young children they were attuned to the responses of children who felt uncomfortable around Liam, and chose their friends accordingly, making life much easier on the family.

It would be natural to feel confused, depressed or stressed by these demands, yet from the outside you wouldn't have gotten the sense Lucinda and Paul were overwhelmed. They got on with the task at hand, reshaping their lives as needed to get through this demanding time. Except for one thing — for many years Lucinda felt a sense of guilt for not providing the opportunities she saw other children had. This guilt was misplaced, she discovered, when one day she asked her children about how they felt about growing up — did they feel they had missed out on holidays or time with their parents, did they feel they had been neglected due to Liam's special needs?

They responded with a resounding no — they had a wonderful, happy childhood and wanted for nothing.

Now that the children are adults Lucinda is reclaiming some personal time, though Liam continues to live at home. Yes, you can have it all, she says, but not all at once.

Lucinda does not for a moment regret her decision to step back. Family has always been her number one priority, and providing the love and support her children needed was paramount. The decision had been easy.

Starting a family totally changed Lucinda's perspective on life. As a parent, children suddenly became the centre of her universe rather than her own personal needs. She also gained perspective on her job — it's important, but just a job in the context of the broader purpose of family. She's certain that being a parent creates greater empathy for the struggles of people doing it tough, especially when you have a child with a disability. She firmly believes this has made her family very mindful of exclusion, of difference and of vulnerability.

The six essentials for success

It's easy to get frustrated trying to balance a career and family responsibility. Here are some pointers inspired by Lucinda's story that will aid in the management of this.

1. *Don't beat yourself up over motherhood guilt or the pursuit of perfection.* Children are adaptable. Do the best you can and don't be hard on yourself. Ask for help when you need it.
2. *Ask for what you need at work.* Parents need a paradoxical combination of flexibility and rigidity in working hours — flexibility to deal with unexpected emergencies, such as a sick child or attending doctors' appointments, and certainty around working hours to plan childcare arrangements. Be clear what you need, ask for it and don't let your manager down.
3. *Seek out advocates.* One of the hallmarks of Lucinda's career has been the intervention, at critical points, of advocates who spotted

her potential, nurtured that potential and provided her with an environment in which her career could continue to flourish. If you have potential and perform well, you will attract advocates.

4. *Work for leaders open to change.* Individual managers need to be open to exploring ways of managing the work schedules of parents. There isn't one solution for everyone. In fact there are probably as many answers to flexible work arrangements as there are people requesting them. Formal policies and arrangements, such as annualised rosters, 24-hour childcare centres and emergency childcare support, are a start. Leaders who can personalise flexible work practices for their staff hit the sweet spot of productivity.

5. *A critical mass of women in the police force will create lasting change.* The hardcore male culture that has historically defined policing will be shaken once more women are appointed to senior ranks and the novelty factor is removed. One thing is clear: the pipeline of women in the police force has never been stronger and women are becoming more visible at senior ranks.

6. *Having it all.* You can have it all, says Lucinda, but not all at the same time. Being a parent can be the most joyous and rewarding time of your life, and there are times when you need to take a sideways career step and prioritise family. The challenge for individuals is to continue to build their skills during this time so they are ready to accelerate their career when the time is right. The challenge for employers is to provide valuable learning opportunities to retain and optimise their investment in employees.

Lisa Croxford

The Job Share Experiment

Lisa Croxford is a Capability Development Manager with international law firm Herbert Smith Freehills. She has a passion for positive psychology and how it can be applied within organisations to improve our experience of work. In her role in the firm's Learning and Development team she designs and facilitates programs for HSF's lawyers and staff, conducts business coaching, and works on organisational development initiatives across the firm.

Prior to this role, Lisa spent 15 years in legal practice, most recently as a Special Counsel and the National Leader of the Equal Opportunity and Training practice at HSF. In this role, she advised on general employment law issues, and held particular expertise in harassment, discrimination and bullying complaints and litigation.

As well as leading the Equal Opportunity and Training practice, she also held leadership roles in HSF's diversity steering committee and knowledge management. Her legal practice also included several years working at Simmons & Simmons in Hong Kong, and client secondments to organisations including Telstra and Goldman Sachs.

Lisa has also trained as a telephone counsellor with the Post and Ante Natal Depression Association, and holds a Graduate Diploma in Psychology, and a Bachelor of Arts/Law (Honours) from Monash University.

Women in the legal profession

A survey of Victorian women lawyers in 2012 revealed that the vast majority of women (95 percent) have their requests for flexible work approved in full or in part. But when asked about the impact of these flexible work arrangements on their careers, 25 percent said that the arrangement had a negative effect on their chances of promotion and career opportunities, and 18 percent said that the quality of work they were given declined.[1] Lisa Croxford is one woman who defied these odds and achieved a flexible solution that met her family and career needs. Here's how.

It seemed like a good idea at the time

Lisa is a high-achieving, highly educated woman who seemed destined for an outstanding career in law. Her accomplishments are impressive. She grew up in a traditional working-class family — her father was a truck driver, her mother a teacher. They instilled a strong work ethic in Lisa from an early age. 'I have always worked,' she recalls. 'As soon as I was old enough to hold a shovel I'd be going off and seeing if the neighbours needed some mulch put on their garden.'

Yet home life was not idyllic. Her mother had been diagnosed with multiple sclerosis when Lisa was ten years old, and suffered from dementia as a result. Her mother gradually lost the ability to move, to look after herself or to communicate. Most of Lisa's recollections of her mother as she was growing up were therefore of her illness.

After completing high school with flying colours, she became the first in her family to be accepted into a Law Degree at Monash University. Her mother would have been as proud as her father.

Why choose law? Lisa was hard-working, smart and academically inclined, so the obvious path for her was to either choose law or medicine. Having no interest in becoming a doctor, she chose law. She excelled in her academic studies, and in her final year was sought out by one of Melbourne's prestigious top-tier law firms, Freehills, where she took articles. Okay, that sounds like an easy choice; who would say no to such an opportunity? Yet Lisa was to discover that while her head was in law, her heart was following a different path, into human resources (HR).

Unbeknown to Lisa at the time, she picked up an HR discipline later in her career that her mother would have dearly liked to pursue, had she been able. One day Lisa was rummaging around some old papers at home and discovered by chance a university transcript that, to her surprise, belonged to her mother. From this document she discovered something about her mother that her family had never spoken about — she had gone back to university courtesy of the free education offered in Australia during the Whitlam years and obtained an HR qualification.

More than just law

Lisa settled in well at Freehills and liked the partners she worked for. She was able to incorporate her interest in HR with law by settling into the Employee Relations practice area. It was there she met Kate Jenkins, a senior associate at that time who was building a new equal opportunity practice area, which ultimately led to Kate fast-tracking her career to partner. Kate, along with other partners like Tony Wood and Chris Gardner, were instrumental in many opportunities offered to her at Freehills. One of these opportunities was being seconded to Telstra as a second year lawyer — to take on a senior role as Acting Legal Counsel Employee Relations, a role previously held by lawyers much more experienced than her.

The Telstra experience led to a moment of truth for Lisa. Working with a major client undergoing significant cultural change, Lisa was drawn to the challenges and opportunities in the human resources domain, and the opportunity it gave to shape the organisation and influence behaviours in it, rather than respond to 'fix' issues that arose with a legal solution. She concluded from this experience that becoming an in-house corporate lawyer was not for her, and that human resources still had her in its grip.

Freehills was the place where she met Tony, her future husband, on her first working day. Both had chosen law, but neither at the time were slavishly devoted to a career in a law firm. They were both working extremely long hours, which meant big sacrifices in their personal lives. In addition, neither of them relished the prospect of slowly moving up a hierarchical and defined career path to partner with the same punishing work schedule that was expected of them. They wanted a more rounded life and to explore what other opportunities the world had to offer, so both started looking at what else might be out there.

Kite flying

One day at Telstra, Lisa was discussing a legal issue with a lawyer acting for the opposing client. This lawyer was a partner with a leading employment law practice in Hong Kong. She was looking to develop an equal opportunity practice in Hong Kong and asked Lisa if she would be interested in joining her. As the equal opportunity laws in Hong Kong are modelled on the Victorian laws, this was a perfect opportunity for Lisa to apply her skills. Tony and Lisa were young, had not yet started a family and decided working overseas would be a fantastic adventure. Off they went, Lisa with a job, Tony initially without, although he quickly managed to find work as a lawyer before they relocated.

Over their three years in Hong Kong, Tony had decided to leave the legal profession and transition into general management. The obvious first step was to pursue a Masters of Business Administration (MBA) and so Tony applied and was accepted into IMD, a top-ranked business school in Switzerland. Lisa resigned, and the next phase of their life began.

As Lisa was unable to obtain work in Switzerland because of visa restrictions, the couple decided this might be a practical time to start a family — good in theory, but Lisa recalls it was possibly her most challenging year. While she dearly loves her daughter, Mia, the reality of transitioning to a stay-at-home mother hit hard. She was in a foreign country where she could barely speak the language, where she had few friends, lacked the support of family, with a husband who was exhausted from the punishing hours required to get through the MBA ('He was a walking zombie,' she recalls). On top of everything else, her mother passed away during this time. This was a real low point in Lisa's life, and led to the decision in 2005 to come home to the familiarity of family, friends and her broader contact base.

The irresistible lure of Freehills

Lisa had a choice about whether to go back to work or not, but decided to re-establish her career at the first opportunity. Her love of working and her strong professional ambitions made her realise she just wasn't wired for staying at home full-time. Having an independent source of income was also a driving force:

> *'It was never an option for me not to work and not to earn an income. I think it's so important for a woman in a relationship to have her own money coming in and be an equal contributing partner in all aspects of that relationship.'*

Her first stop was Freehills, where she had forged her credentials as a lawyer. She was clear about what she wanted — to resurrect her legal career, but to do so around the responsibilities of family life. Lisa thought the way to manage this was to ask for a two-day-a-week, non-fee-earning role. Lisa met with Chris Gardner, who (likely after consultation with other partners, including Kate and Tony) took her back, but on the basis that a fee-earning role was possible. Lisa could not recall any other part-timer who worked in a fee-earning role, and wasn't sure how it would work. However, she was committed to making it a success, even though she thinks back on that time as a difficult one:

> *'They really didn't know what to do with me — and I didn't either. There were no precedents for this. I had some days where I was walking to work asking myself, "Seriously, what am I coming in for because there's not really much here for me to do."'*

Why wasn't Lisa more assertive and authoritative, and why didn't she speak up and demand more challenging work at the time? Perhaps the answer lay in the tug of war going on in her mind between wanting to give 100 percent to a demanding job, and the pull of mothering. She didn't want to put success in the office ahead of the demands and rewards of parenting Mia, and felt she was struggling to pursue both well. By this stage Tony was working for a top-tier management consulting firm and was on a gruelling schedule of extensive travel and long working hours. Lisa couldn't imagine committing to a demanding career while simultaneously taking the lion's share of parenting. Also, she and Tony were thinking of having another child, requiring another career interruption for her.

This is often a confusing time in many women's lives, and Lisa is not alone in having these doubts. She observes other women at a similar stage experiencing torn loyalties — having just become a mother, they are discovering a new identity for themselves, often feeling conflicted in their ability to give 100 percent to their multiple roles as mother, wife and career woman.

A win-win-win

Jack was born around 12 months after Lisa returned to work. While on parental leave, Tony Wood, a senior partner in the employment law practice, gave her the opportunity to work on a short-term project, writing 'Know How' guides for lawyers in the practice. This was a perfect assignment for Lisa. She could retain ties with the firm, work more predictable and manageable hours, and at the same time up-skill her own knowledge on employment law, having been out of the country for several years. While on parental leave she was promoted to senior associate.

She returned to work around the same time as another female senior associate, Trish Low, was returning from parental leave. Tony Wood saw this as an opportunity to trial a job share arrangement. It was great timing for both of them, and they were determined to make it work.

Lisa attributes the success of the job share experiment to several factors. Firstly, she and Trish were like-minded in their commitment to client service above all else, and wished to preserve their strong professional reputation. They were both highly detail-oriented and perfectionists when it came to their work. They fully debriefed each other at changeover times and kept in touch when needed. They copied in their supervising partners on these handover emails, and these partners would frequently comment to them how detailed the handovers were (and would sometimes use it as a 'quick cheat' if they had lost track of where a matter was up to). If anything went wrong Trish and Lisa were adamant it wouldn't be blamed on the job share arrangement not working out.

Secondly, Trish and Lisa addressed the work through multiple lenses. This included the client's needs and when the work needed to be done. But it also included an understanding of each other's strengths and areas for development. One of the bonuses they realised about job sharing that was not apparent from the start was the immense opportunity it gave to learn from each other. Lisa recalls Trish had a real discipline around planning client events, and while Lisa might ordinarily (if she was working on her own) drag her feet, Trish would organise it and put them on track. This motivated Lisa to then meet Trish's expectations and not let her down! Something that is also hugely important with job sharing is attacking the work with an absence of ego. Their arrangement would never have worked if they each tried to compete with each other for the best work, or the best client, or to avoid the difficult parts of legal practice (reviewing bills, having 'difficult' conversations with people in the team). They would review what needed to be done, and then discuss who was best placed (in all senses) to do that work.

Thirdly, they recognised they needed to address some doubters in the firm. Kate Jenkins reflects that Lisa and Trish played the role of 'myth-busters', as they were aware many partners believed job sharing would not work, fearing it would inconvenience them, deliver lower quality work and not meet client expectations. Client feedback, however, demonstrated that the job share arrangement was a resounding success. Lisa and Trish proved all of those fears wrong, says Kate, and built a strong and respected legal practice as a team. Partners were then able to advocate for job share with external clients based on their personal experience. Freehills was able to position itself as a leader in practising what it preached in diversity and flexible work practices — a win for everyone.

Fourthly, having male and female senior advocates in the firm helped greatly. Kate Jenkins was a role model for a successful partner with children working part-time, and having access to Kate enabled Lisa to discuss challenges around integrating career and motherhood in confidential conversations. Tony Wood also made as many adjustments as needed to ensure she could return to work in a fulfilling and flexible role.

Finally, and perhaps most importantly, flexibility on both sides was important — both Lisa's and the firm's. She would make herself available on her non-working days for urgent matters by phone or email, and always endeavoured to return phone calls promptly when she was not in the office. Small things also mattered, for example, she decided not to post an automatic out-of-office notification on her email on days she wasn't working so that clients — especially those not used to working with her — never doubted her ability to meet their needs. At the same time she resisted the pull of partners pressuring her to physically come into the office on her days off.

Second time around is easier

Being a mum for the second time was so much easier than the first. The first time, Lisa was riddled with anxiety about how it was going to work, especially being overseas without a support system in place. Second time around, she learned to relax and accept that uncertainty about some things was okay. She was also very deliberate about organising a network of support, including insisting her husband take four weeks parental leave and sharing the parenting responsibilities at home. She also found that sticking to her guns about what was important to her, in developing her legal practice as an equal opportunity specialist, and in maintaining space for family and study, paid off. In 2010, Lisa was promoted to Special Counsel.

Tony now manages a team of managers, many of whom are women. Lisa strongly encourages Tony to model for his staff the way to handle both a career and parenting, and demonstrate (and understand) that, through his involvement in shared parenting, he is juggling the same responsibilities and challenges they face.

Exploring her real passion

After having Jack, Lisa was clearer about her desire to move out of a legal career and explore her real passion: human resources. When Jack was six months old she went back to university and completed a Graduate Diploma in Psychology. 'It was completely nuts in hindsight,' she recalls, studying on top of managing two children and a part-time job. She then completed a coaching qualification. The partners were supportive of her studying, and Lisa believes they likely never considered Lisa would leave legal practice — 'In their way they wondered why you would want to do anything else. There's nothing better than being a Freehills employment lawyer!'

Around the same time, Kate Jenkins was presented with an amazing opportunity, to apply for the role of the Victorian Equal Opportunity and Human Rights Commissioner. Kate was successful in obtaining the role. Lisa was asked to take Kate's place as Practice Leader of the Equal Opportunity & Training Practice, on a three day a week arrangement, supported by Trish Low. In that role she led the firm's equal opportunity and workplace training practice, and was a key advisor to the firm's HR team on employment law.

Lisa was now at what she felt was the pinnacle of an equal opportunity practice at the leading employment law firm in Australia, but she was not satisfied. The next step was partnership, an incredibly competitive and demanding path to pursue, especially given the complex and changing landscapes of global law firms. Years of hard work, pressure and personal sacrifices would be required to make it, and for a prize that ultimately did not embody her growing passion and interests. While never afraid of hard work, Lisa realised that while partnership was seen as the ultimate success for many lawyers, it wasn't what success meant for her. She loved the people she worked with, but she didn't love the practice of law or the management of a legal practice, and for her that meant the sacrifices weren't worth it. She might be successful in the eyes of other lawyers, but she (and likely her family) would be miserable.

Lisa went back to her vision of a life outside of legal practice, and armed with qualifications she'd built in psychology and coaching, as well as her experience in employment law and training, reached out to her networks to explore opportunities in HR outside Herbert Smith Freehills and was contemplating a role with another top-tier law firm. The Australia Head of HR at Herbert Smith Freehills discovered that Lisa was looking around, and asked what she required in order to stay.

In May 2014, Lisa started a new role at Herbert Smith Freehills in their learning and development team. In that role she coaches, develops and mentors legal staff at all levels — a perfect blend of law and human resources disciplines. A real joy in Lisa's new role is coaching women around the firm who have a passion for the law and want to achieve success in their careers, and balance this with their personal lives (whatever that 'balance' might mean for them).

Ongoing challenges with creating true flexibility

Ten years after Lisa returned to Herbert Smith Freehills, diversity and inclusion is in full swing. In March 2014, the firm announced a 30 percent gender target for the proportion of women in its global partnership. In May 2015, 22 percent of its partners in Australia are women, and 20 percent globally. The 2015 Australia partner promotions saw six new partners appointed, four of whom are women.

And all four work part-time and were promoted while working part-time, a first for the firm. Two non-executive appointments were also recently made to the firm's Global Council, and both are also women.

Herbert Smith Freehills was awarded Employer of Choice for Women by the Equal Opportunity for Women in the Workplace Agency (EOWA) for six consecutive years (2006–2012) and Best Law Firm for lesbian, gay, bisexual, transgendered and intersex (LGBTI) workplace inclusion in 2014. Tony Wood also won the Executive Leadership Award for LGBTI Workplace Inclusion. The firm also provides a very generous Paid Parental Leave policy of 18 weeks, plus superannuation. This is available to any primary carer of a newborn (including via a surrogacy arrangement) or newly adopted child, regardless of that parent's gender.

Many large law firms still grapple with flexibility. Some partners or managers don't fully understand or are uncomfortable with how flexible arrangements can work. There's an experience gap with some of these partners and managers — men and women — who have experienced or are experiencing 'traditional' Australian family models of having a partner, typically a wife, taking care of the family and managing the household. It limits their experience and they often can't see a way of working flexibly or sustainably for women or men (who are also increasingly seeking to pursue flexible roles). Perhaps greater understanding and accommodation of flexible needs will emerge as more partners have life partners who are also pursuing careers and require flexibility.

There are still too few women partners in law firms. The difficulty for many young female lawyers wishing to make partner is that the partnership carrot is being dangled in front of them provided they work a punishing schedule. They know they have limited time, from a biological viewpoint, to have children — slap bang in the middle of their promotable years — so they delay it and succumb to the long hours regime demanded of them.

Unconscious bias is also at play. Many still adhere to a kind of blokey male culture and behaviour. The message they send is that the only way to succeed is to work extreme hours to the exclusion of all else. Lisa recalls being asked by a great supporter of flexible hours: 'Are you still working part-time?' The comment was meant well, but the underlying implication was that part-time work is just a short-term solution or special arrangement rather than a legitimate way of working.

Lisa is passionate about raising awareness of the bystander effect,[2] in which individuals do not offer support to a victim when other people are present. It plays out in the workplace in many ways, such as 'harmless jokes', sexual harassment comments, or off-hand remarks to part-timers about their commitment to the firm and their careers. If these behaviours are not challenged, inappropriate behaviour is then either deemed acceptable or snowballs out of control, and it affects the decisions women are making in these firms about whether to stay or whether to pursue a fulfilling, successful career elsewhere. Part of the conundrum is about power imbalance — if a senior partner is going to make a remark, it takes guts for a junior associate to challenge them.

Advice to younger lawyers

Lisa observes other young women facing similar dilemmas and challenges that she's had to work through and offers them the following advice:

1. *Be clear about your vision, values and direction.* Understand what will work for you. It could include staying at home or returning to work.
2. *Once you're clear about your direction, develop a plan to get there.* Arrange your family life around your direction and constantly assess situations, dilemmas and decision points around your values, especially those situations you will face in balancing competing demands of work and home.
3. *Manage boundaries and hold firm.* If you're working part-time

there will be times when you need to push back on pressure to work longer hours or come in on non-work days, but also assure partners and clients you'll be available when needed over phone/email for urgent calls.

4. *Prove that it can work.* Do everything you can to ensure your flexible work arrangements are a success. You may need to overcome biases and the concerns of managers who have never experienced a part-time person working for them. You may have to go above and beyond the call of duty at times, to ensure you have met your clients' needs.

5. *Don't struggle on your own.* Share your concerns with other women experiencing the same situation. Motherhood guilt, for example, is something almost all women grapple with. Sharing the problem normalises your feelings and helps you identify strategies for overcoming your concerns.

6. *Be courageous in asking for what you need.* Advocate for what you need in the language that a law firm partner understands. If you are a valued and high performing member of the team, your manager won't want to lose you and will generally try to accommodate your needs. Lisa believes any role can be performed part-time with the support of the manager.

7. *Actively explore job share options.* More and more lawyers are working part-time. Find out who these people are, talk about job share, and be flexible in your thinking. If that person has a similar working style to you, but a slightly different practice area, how might you arrange a job share arrangement that gives you the flexibility you need as well as experience in a new area of law? It may end up a win-win, flexibility in the short term, greater breadth of experience and client contacts in the long term, to launch your future success.

8. *Find a mentor to advocate for you.* Like Lisa, many successful leaders have had mentors who played an active and critical role

in their career progression. Mentors advocate for you in critical meetings, raise your profile among key decision-makers and identify opportunities for you to grow and develop, as well as being your own trusted advisor at critical times.

9. *Don't be a bystander.* Call out inappropriate behaviour or ask someone else to do so if you feel you lack the power to challenge those in authority. (And don't assume that one person's attitude to women and flexible work are the views of the organisation.) By allowing poor behaviour to continue unchecked you are reinforcing a culture that undermines the progress of everyone, including women.

Are partnerships different?

The globalisation of law practices such as Herbert Smith Freehills places unique challenges on partners in addressing the work-life conundrum. Profits per partner continue to be the litmus test in most top-tier law firms, judged annually by league tables published in the *Australian Financial Review*, and other publications. Where does this leave the work-life balance? If local partners want to create a firm that helps lawyers to be exceptional but in a sustainable way around their personal lives, perhaps there is a knock-on effect for profitability. It's time some firms began this type of conversation, Lisa believes.

> *'Large law firms hold a real dissonance on this. They are saying to women, "You are important to us, we want to keep you. We'll make that flexibility work." But actually to succeed here it's often about the hours that you put in.'*

Lisa reflects that things are changing, however, and she is optimistic about the future for women, and men, at the firm. Many of the strategies put in place over the last five years are starting to come to fruition and Lisa has observed firsthand how the senior leadership team is absolutely dedicated to tackling these issues. The firm tracks the success of women throughout all stages of their career, and if the numbers don't add up, are asking why. Lisa concludes:

> *'We're talking about unconscious bias with our partners, and witnessing them calling each other on it. There are partners who are having quality conversations with their lawyers that embrace discussions about their hopes for their personal lives and families, to help them to then plan their career accordingly. The more we do that as an organisation, the better we will become.'*

Several smaller firms have been leading the way for some time already. Take the highly successful employment law firm Justitia, profiled in *Sideways To The Top*.[3] The firm's approach is based on the provision of exemplary client service delivered in a totally unique way — no billable hours, targets or budgets for individual lawyers, and clients are served through teamwork and collaboration across the legal practice, rather than relying on a relationship with one partner. Working flexible hours is part of the DNA at Justitia and has helped create a culture of success. Justitia was named Law Firm of the Year in 2013 by the Law Institute of Victoria, and in 2014 was presented with the Australian Human Resources Institute's Award for Workplace Flexibility.

Another law firm making great strides in achieving gender equity is Melbourne law firm Maddocks. Women comprise 31 percent of its partnership, way above the industry average of 23 percent, thanks to the implementation of several innovative and flexible work practices to support their female senior associates and partners. For instance, during maternity leave the firm appoints 'a custodian partner' to manage matters and clients, then transitions these clients back to the senior associate or partner when they return. They also provide budget relief and specific marketing support for a period of 12 months after their return to assist them in re-establishing their practice.[4]

Beyond a women's issue

Ultimately, a career model for law firms based on long hours in the office, brutal travel schedules, working across a range of time zones and the constant pressure of time-based billable hours, marginalises and derails talented people juggling work and family responsibilities. This goes beyond being just a women's issue. These punishing work schedules wreak havoc in the private lives of everyone, and undermine the health and wellbeing of all staff.

There will always be law firms that persist with this model of work, just as there will always be ambitious people prepared to work in this one-dimensional way. There is not one model of success; the problem lies with not addressing the challenges and opportunities diversity presents. Law firms who are unable or unwilling to accommodate other ways of operating will lose talented men and women to a competitor who better understands and can respond to the different and complex needs of their staff. Imaginative solutions abound for those leaders who seek it out.

Jodie Sizer

When Passions Collide

Jodie Sizer is a Djap Wurrung/Gunditjmara woman, and part of the Framlingham Community of South West Victoria. Jodie is a Co-owner Principal of PwC's Indigenous Consulting, a new member firm in the PwC global network.

Previously she was the Principal Consultant and Director of Ingenuity Australia, a consulting group that provides leadership, development and project management skills to Indigenous communities.

Jodie was named as Victorian Aboriginal Young Achiever in 2000, when she was working as an auditor at a Big Four accounting firm, and has maintained a prominent role in the Indigenous space and across broader society.

Jodie has also worked in Indigenous organisations and government. She was an ATSIC Regional Councillor, a finalist in the Telstra Business Women of the Year Award, listed in the Who's Who of Australian Women publication, inducted on the Victorian Women's Honour Roll, recipient of the Prime Ministers Centenary Medal and listed as one of the *Australian Financial Review*'s 100 Women of Influence.

Labour of love

I head up to PwC's swish corporate offices in Freshwater Place and meet with a woman with striking good looks, warm charm and a disarming frankness. She is close to tears, but smiling during our first encounter. 'I still tear up, as you can see, at least once a week,' she says, describing her battle with managing the competing demands of full-time work and family.

With three daughters — Chloe, one year old, Tia, three years old, and Elleischa, the big sister at six years old — Jodie is in the throes of early parenting, riding the emotional roller-coaster that many women embark on when work loyalties collide with family commitments.

Why does Jodie put herself through the stress, the sacrifice of her own personal time, the long hours away from her family, the heart-wrenching moments of missing her girls, and the associated guilt?

The irresistible magnetic pull of her past

For clues to the forces that put the fire in Jodie's belly, we need to explore her upbringing and childhood influences.

Jodie was born in the mid-1970s, a Djab Wurrung/Gunditjmara woman, and the oldest of five children. She came from a family of battlers. Her father was raised on an Aboriginal mission station at Framlingham in Western Victoria. He was a ward of the State from a young age, in and out of prison, as Jodie informs me, a fierce advocate for his mob. Jodie's mother was born and raised in Warrnambool. Jodie grew up in a housing commission estate in Ballarat.

While Jodie was at primary school, her parents separated. During Year 12, at age 16, she left home. Tough times, she recalls, but you just have to get on with life, even if you're still a teenager. Her first encounter with the tertiary sector didn't go well. She commenced a university degree, but immediately felt a sense of exclusion and the target of racism. After failing her first year, she left and transferred to a TAFE college to complete a Certificate in Banking and Finance.

In some ways, Jodie is her father's daughter. She sees herself continuing the unfinished business of his advocacy work within the Aboriginal community, achieving better outcomes for her mob, locally and on a national 'game-changing scale'.

Yet it took time for Jodie to reach this point. It was when she began working in a local Aboriginal cooperative, in her teenage years, that she became further engaged in conversations around the history of her people, understood the injustices perpetrated on them and began to realise the impact of these events on their lives, and her own life. These conversations eventually set an entire series of events in motion. She began to realise her identity as an Aboriginal woman, and developed a strong conviction that her purpose in life was integrally bound up with righting the injustices her people had suffered, and wanting to help improve the lives of Aboriginal people. Her relationship with her father became stronger during this time.

When the funding for her job at the Aboriginal cooperative ceased, a friend encouraged her to return to university and, after overcoming her hesitation, she enrolled in a Bachelor of Accounting.

The second time around was a totally different experience. Being a more mature student, Jodie enjoyed study and excelled academically, receiving distinctions and high distinctions. She connected with the Aboriginal community on and around campus, encouraging Aboriginal children to consider a university degree, and taking on the role of support worker for Aboriginal students.

In her final year, Ernst & Young's recruitment team approached her. 'We want the cream of the crop,' they told her, 'and if you work for us, you can become a partner earning a starting salary of $250,000 per year.' This was a fortune for Jodie, who had identified her dream salary to be a modest $1000 per week. 'People earn that much?' she thought. 'That's my life, I'm ready.' She was totally mesmerised by this prestigious top-tier accounting firm and the opportunities they offered. Naturally, she accepted.

At Ernst & Young she found the position of auditor enjoyable, easy and a good fit with her skills, but not entirely satisfying — she much preferred working with people than with balance sheets. So she volunteered for several committees, and was in turn awarded Aboriginal Young Achiever of the Year for Victoria. This award provided the opportunity to attend the United Nations in Geneva, and provided enormous opportunity for her to pursue her dream of advocacy. She realised she lacked the aspiration required to fit the Ernst & Young culture — the long hours in the office and complete dedication to the firm — so she told her manager she wanted to leave. 'To be honest,' she said to her manager, 'I'd rather be the Commissioner or Chairperson of the Aboriginal and Torres Strait Islander Commission.' Little did she know that within a few years she would indeed become an ATSIC Councillor, and that the detour she took to work at Ernst & Young would prove invaluable later in life.

Success redefined

'What is success? It is being able to go to bed each night with your soul at peace.'
— Paulo Coelho

No longer striving to become a $250,000 a year partner with Ernst & Young, she was driven by the prospect of correcting the wrongs of the past and supporting Aboriginal people to realise their social, economic and political potential. For the next three years, Jodie worked in government as an Aboriginal business development advisor, helping Aboriginal communities identify and develop business ideas. She also put herself through a Certified Practicing Accountant program. It soon became clear that she was overqualified for an advisor role and could make more of a difference to her people by starting her own consulting firm, Ingenuity Australia. This business was part of a larger franchise.

This was a great time in Jodie's career, spanning eight years. With a small team of Aboriginal staff connected by the same beliefs, values and objectives, she worked on projects that impacted at a local level, and had the autonomy and flexibility to work in her own authentic way.

During the latter part of these years, Jodie and her husband moved from Melbourne to Brisbane. At 34 years of age, she had their first child, Elleischa. This was the height of Jodie's career, she recalls — the firm had a great reputation for quality work, it was financially very profitable and she was involved in a range of committees that enabled her to pursue her passion for activism. She also achieved the perfect balance between work and family during this time, a balance that she is today fervently trying to regain.

Small business has its drawbacks, however, with limited capacity to work on significant projects and with the constraints a franchise brings. Ultimately, she felt she couldn't continue with the franchise and terminated the agreement, at great financial expense but with her integrity intact.

A balanced life

Balance for Jodie back in those days meant enjoying life as a mother, working three days a week with a small team of fantastic people, and being able to pick and choose the work and the hours she wanted. Elleischa integrated seamlessly into Jodie's work life, sitting on her lap in meetings, travelling with her and being around for much of Jodie's day.

Having a second child was a real game-changer, recalls Jodie. Suddenly she had to accommodate a toddler and a baby, so integrating them into her workday became problematic. From that point on they hired a nanny, three days a week, which worked exceptionally well. Before long Jodie was pregnant with their third child.

Jodie had planned to take 12 months off work after she exited the franchise business, to spend time with her family and enjoy being a mother. But PwC approached her to start up an Indigenous consulting business, and the opportunity was too good to turn down. After 12 months of tough soul-searching with her family, and countless meetings with PwC to thrash out the details, PwC's Indigenous Consulting (PIC) was born. PwC owns 49 percent of PIC, giving Jodie and her partners the majority shareholding and ultimate decision-making authority.

A once-in-a-lifetime opportunity

PIC focuses on strengthening Aboriginal communities through the provision of professional services. This includes providing advice directly to the communities, and to businesses and government wishing to engage with Indigenous Australia. Jodie is convinced that co-founding a consulting firm with one of the world's largest professional services firms is a once-in-a-lifetime opportunity to realise her dream of creating significant and lasting change for her people. With a team of 30 consultants (65 percent of staff are Aboriginal), which will grow to 40 in 2016, and having the immense pool of talent of 6000 people across PwC Australia on hand, PIC can achieve outcomes at a significantly deeper level than Jodie ever could have in a smaller consulting practice. Living out her purpose in a meaningful and lasting way makes the juggling and sacrifice worth it — and for the most part she is really enjoying the challenge.

However, if she could've chosen the timing, it wouldn't have been in 2013. Jodie was pregnant with her third child, Chloe, while she was in negotiations with PwC, who was three months old when the partnership began.

Jodie commenced work on a three day a week arrangement, but soon this climbed to four days, then full-time. Establishing a successful business was not a part-time enterprise, as Jodie was discovering. On top of the gruelling hours and 90-minute commute to and from work every day, she had experienced the full roller-coaster of emotions of any parent — at the end of the day, she simply missed her children and couldn't wait to be with them again. At the end of her first year she says she 'felt like a pile of human mush; I was just so exhausted'.

Many women may relate to the conflict of passions and motherhood guilt she experiences on a daily basis. Jodie reveals that 'every time I leave the house I feel guilty and every time I'm away I worry about what I'm going to miss.' She recalls specific times with her girls that are deeply moving:

> *'I felt overwhelmed with guilt when I attended Elleischa's ballet concert, guilty that I hadn't been part of it, that I hadn't been able to take Elleischa to ballet every week. When Elleischa was at school we used to have Mummy and Tia days. Tia asks for Mummy and Tia days every week and it breaks my heart.*
>
> *Will I feel like I've missed out on a whole lot of things between now and when Chloe starts school in four years' time? I don't know.'*

She still has daily conversations with herself about getting the balance right. She leaves home before the children wake up, and returns home in time for dinner. She also aims to spend Wednesdays working from home. At PwC everyone is measured on their output and the value they bring to the firm. A flexible workday/workplace is encouraged. She also encourages others in her team to find schedules that work for their families and personal circumstances.

Deep down she knows she will excel at PwC as well as raise three beautiful daughters, whom she describes as 'incredibly healthy, gorgeous and ridiculously happy'. Ultimately, being a mum is the most important thing she will ever do.

Someone to watch over us

Having a supportive and available husband was crucial when Jodie commenced at PIC. She describes Chris's first foray into parenting as 'coming from ground zero, domestically illiterate', with no idea how much detail goes into managing the minutiae of the household. He's a fast learner though, and his relationship with the girls has absolutely deepened and strengthened since he has taken on a larger slice of the parenting responsibilities. His pragmatism and military precision (he comes from an Army background) balances out Jodie's emotional reactions, so as a team they combine their diverse talents to make it work. Fortunately, Chris works close to home, and his job allows some flexibility in terms of hours to accommodate the needs and schedules of the family.

A backup plan for emergencies and school holidays is essential. Things can go off the rails very quickly, like when Chris had his first pick-up and forgot school finished at 3pm and not 3.30pm, or missing the odd birthday party or forgetting to get the bread on the way home.

There is a very strong local mothers and friends network, for which the couple are very grateful. But it also has its challenges — Jodie is sure there are judgmental views held by some, and acknowledges it's not for everyone.

> *'Some mums say to me: "How can you do it? How can you work?" I almost feel like saying to them: "How can you not have a career? To realise your own potential and to do something really meaningful, improving the lives of others who are less fortunate, in the short time we have in our lives — why would you not want to do that?"'*

Jodie and Chris's backup plan includes Franny Nanny, the neighbours, her brother, sister, or mother if absolutely necessary. Jodie has learnt to ask for help.

Having a third child is 'massive', says Jodie. You're switched on 24/7, but suddenly you can lose control. On the mornings when Jodie is at home, a typical morning will be filled with Jodie breastfeeding Chloe and trying to express milk, dealing with Chloe's teething, preparing Elleischa for school and Tia for childcare, and dealing with any disputes, emotions and tears. The afternoons are organised like a military operation, with Chris picking the children up from childcare and school, preparing dinner, feeding and bathing them, then Jodie coming home for dinner and to spend time with the girls. When she's home, Jodie is fully committed to being available for them, being more aware of what is going on in their lives, talking through emotional issues and giving them certainty about when Mum will be home. Jodie will often leave for work early in the morning before the girls are awake, to minimise the stress on both sides. Interstate travel adds another layer of complexity, with the girls missing her more keenly at this time. They need certainty about when she'll be home, when they'll see her and when she'll be away.

Recharge and renew

In this child-centric family, the couple's time alone together has all but vanished. In the past, Jodie and Chris may have sat down together in the evening for a long conversation, or they might have spontaneously gone out for dinner and a movie, perhaps met with similarly footloose friends. These days, when they're lucky, they might get an hour or two alone after an exhausting evening. More likely, they'll both fall into bed exhausted, recognising that the morning will bring a recurrent schedule of frantic activity before heading off to childcare, school and work. Weekends are also totally dedicated to time with the girls.

Their relationship is strong and they delight in having their children around, but parenting three young girls has reinforced the need for some child-free time together. It's unlikely to happen spontaneously at home, so the challenge is to schedule 'date nights' and ensure they remain sacrosanct. For the time being it's all about quality, not quantity.

Jodie recognises that reconnecting with her Aboriginal history plays a vital role of renewal. Being part of her Aboriginal community and fulfilling her responsibilities is also a very important part of Jodie's wellbeing. She is committed to participating in Aboriginal ceremonies and events to ensure she and her family continue to connect with the spiritual, cultural and religious traditions of the Wurrung/Gunditjmara.

Making decisions

Jodie's story shows the stark reality of what a person goes through to become a mother: how much it costs, how much energy it takes, and how to hold true to your belief systems. Jodie doesn't have the answers — she's learning through trial and error, like most mothers. Parenting books are not that much help, she has found. As her mother reminded her: 'The kids don't write the books, Jodie. You just have to listen to your child and figure it out.'

She understands what's important for each of her girls and for the family. She's clear about how to be the mum *she* wants to be, rather than trying to live up to other people's expectations, and makes her choices accordingly.

Ultimately, she falls back on Tony Soprano's quote from the television series *The Sopranos*: 'A wrong decision is better than indecision.' It's agonising for Jodie to be in that space of indecision; she'll make her decisions and be happy with them.

Tracey Spicer

Fearlessness

Tracey Spicer is one of the most versatile journalists and presenters in the country, with a portfolio spanning television, radio, newspapers, magazines, and online media. During her 27-year career, she has anchored news, current affairs and lifestyle programs in Sydney, Melbourne and Brisbane.

Currently, Tracey works as an anchor for Sky News, weekly columnist for Fairfax Media and Debrief Daily, cast member of ABC TV's *Agony* series, and presentation trainer at the Australian Film, Television and Radio School.

She is best known for presenting Channel Ten's national weekend and morning news services for 14 years.

Tracey has written, produced and presented documentaries for NGOs in Bangladesh, Kenya, Papua New Guinea, and India.

The mother of two is an Ambassador for ActionAid, World Vision, Life's Little Treasures, Aspect, and Dying with Dignity, Patron of the NSW Cancer Council and the National Premmie Foundation, and face of the Garvan Institute's research into pancreatic cancer.

As you'd probably guess from her Twitter feed, Tracey is passionate about women's rights, social justice, and equal opportunity, and a lobbyist for the voluntary euthanasia movement.

The 48-year-old has just set up Women in Media, a mentoring and networking group, backed by the Media Entertainment and Arts Alliance.

Commercial media is gradually moving on from the opulence, chauvinism and sexism that characterised it in the 1980s. Gone are the big budgets, the limitless opportunities to be bold, the extravagant events and the stereotypical weather girl. These days it's more about cost-cutting, downsizing, quick news bites and instant updates. Nevertheless, commercial media still has a long way to go when it comes to eliminating sexism and recognising women in executive ranks.

Women journalism graduates outnumber men, yet according to research conducted by New Matilda, no woman edits a major daily newspaper, 23 out of 24 CEOs are men, only 15 percent of Board members in private media companies are women (compared to 50 percent on the ABC Board and 55 percent on the SBS Board) and men hold 14 out of 15 Chairperson roles.[1] New Matilda rightly poses the question: Where have all the women gone?

In this chapter we explore the experiences of Tracey Spicer, who experienced momentous and unplanned career interruptions, and prevailed.

Fearless

Tracey Spicer knows more than most about a woman's highs and lows in media. She has always been a formidable newsreader, feisty and direct, not afraid to push the boundaries and agitate for what she believes in. Her supporters were shocked when she was brutally dumped from Channel Ten by the men in power. Since then she has leapt into social media with gusto, brilliantly resurrecting her career as a successful commentator and thought leader across traditional and digital media.

Tracey buzzes with energy when we start our conversation. Her family background provided a good grounding for journalism. Her feminist convictions and social justice values were set during her early years growing up in Redcliffe, a working-class suburb on the outskirts of Brisbane. Her mother, she recalls, was opinionated and a strong feminist; her father a social justice warrior. The family thrived on a good argument.

Tracey had clarity early in life about the direction her career would take. Her curiosity, her desire to get to the bottom of a story and her passion to represent battlers could have led her down the paths of either law or journalism. Journalism won when she saw Jana Wendt reading the news.

After completing a Bachelor of Business in Communications at the Queensland University of Technology, Tracey moved up and down the Eastern seaboard to gain breadth of experience. She went from Brisbane to Melbourne and Sydney, from radio (3AW) to regional and commercial television (Channel Nine and Ten).

She recalls that about 97 percent of graduates in her year were women. Looking at women in the media now, she feels like a whole generation of them has simply gone missing. These women, who should now be in middle to upper management, are simply not there.

In her early days of journalism at 3AW, she was only one of two women police reporters in Melbourne. She was fearless, investigating and reporting on tough underworld crime stories during the lead up to the Walsh Street police killings. She recalls a time when a member of the elite police force's Special Operations Group tackled her at two o'clock in the morning after she stumbled into a siege. Those were the days when reporters could listen to police scanners, jump out of bed and chase the story.

Standing up to the brat pack

Her experience with career and motherhood was very different to Jen's, to say the least. She worked in a culture where it was considered sport to target women, enduring comments such as: 'You only need to be in this job for a couple of years, then you'll marry a nice rich businessman and you'll never have to work again.' She recalls being asked during a contract negotiation at Channel Ten if she was planning on starting a family. She replied, 'Well yes, actually, we're trying to have kids now.' Ever since that moment, she heard the sound of doors being slammed shut and opportunities just not being offered to her anymore. She suffered through the blokey culture for years, and had seen many of her female journalist friends experience great difficulty in balancing children and a career, so she put off having children as long as possible.

Tracey was a presenter of the national weekend news and mid-morning bulletin, when she found out she was pregnant with her first child, Taj, at age 37. She thought she knew what to expect from work, yet she was unprepared for the brutality of management's response when it came. Her pregnancy had life-threatening complications, which meant she had to give up work five and a half months into her confinement. Her boss was unsympathetic, not wanting her off air for such a long period of time.

But Tracey was determined. The obvious signs that they didn't want her back in her former role came through random phone calls to the effect of: 'When you come back you'll probably want to go behind the scenes anyway,' meaning, of course, to a lower-paid, lower-profile role. Unlikely!

She returned to work after three months to be told that her current roster would be offered to some younger presenters. Having researched her legal rights before the meeting she was well prepared, and threatened to take legal action if the station attempted to move her out of her role.

After standing up to her boss, she felt she was subsequently treated 'like a piece of dirt on his shoe, which is what I expected'. She was being told she was 'porking up', she was 'getting a bit long in the tooth and shouldn't she go behind the scenes?' She claims the station made her roster very difficult for her, hoping she would leave, changing her hours so she would finish at midnight on Sunday night and return at seven o'clock on Monday morning.

However, she was determined to make it work. The culture of misogyny seemed intractable, but Tracey was a fighter.

From reading the news to becoming the news

While she was still breastfeeding Taj, Tracey unexpectedly fell pregnant with her second child, Grace. She had planned to take ten weeks maternity leave after her birth, but eight weeks in she received a phone call from Channel Ten urging her to come back early to start up a new bulletin. She went back, relieved that she had a job at all.

Four weeks later, she grabbed the headlines herself when she was sacked via email. Not one to slink away quietly into the shadows or submissively agree to resign 'for family reasons', she took legal action, alleging breaches of the Sex Discrimination Act and Trade Practices Act. She signed off for the final time on New Year's Eve 2006, after 14 years with Channel Ten. Four days later she began working for Sky News.

Tracey's career has now blossomed. As well as being an anchor on Sky News, she is a weekly columnist for Fairfax Media and Debrief Daily, a radio broadcaster and presentation trainer at the Australian Film, Television and Radio School. She founded a communications business, Spicer Communications, and recently established Women in Media, a mentoring and networking group. She is a prolific contributor on social media websites and Twitter.

The most exciting part of this story is that her new career began at a time when the traditional media was on the wane and social media was emerging as the new powerhouse for communications. Social media platforms are democratising communication, giving everyone, regardless of gender, age or circumstance, huge and unfettered opportunities to express their views and contribute to debates in the communities of their choosing. Tracey will no doubt be at the forefront once social media grows in influence. What perfect timing.

Being a mum

Becoming a mother, reflects Tracey, was both the hardest and most wonderful thing she has ever done. She was, however, unprepared for the day-to-day reality of switching her identity. Imagine a high-profile public figure interviewing business leaders and politicians one moment, and cleaning up poo, heating up bottles and dealing with a crying baby the next!

Tracey's husband is a genuine 50/50 parent and they work together like a well-oiled machine, chuckles Tracey. He took three months parental leave after Taj was born. As the head of the camera department at Network Ten, he was able to juggle shifts to work around family needs.

Tracey believes she has become a better journalist after becoming a mother. She now has shared experiences and much greater empathy with working families, and is organised down to the second and much more productive at work.

Insights

Tracey's stories, experiences and reactions indicate a person who stands her ground when it matters, drawing on her values and personal principles to guide her decisions. Tracey has never let stereotypes about what women should do get in the way of her career success. This fearlessness in the face of adversity gives all of us courage.

I was intrigued to hear Tracey's insights into some of the pressing questions women in the media face.

When is the right time to have a child?

Medically, the best age to fall pregnant is between 20 and 35 years, when women are most fertile. Yet women are delaying motherhood for many reasons. Some choose to establish their career first, want to ensure financial security or may have only found a partner later in life. Whatever the reason, the average age of first-time mothers is currently 28.4 years and the number of older women having children has tripled over the last 30 years.[2]

Tracey notes that barriers still exist, especially for women. When coaching women in media today they often ask her for advice about when to start a family, still believing they are going to be relegated to lesser roles when they return to work. Clarify your priorities and timing, and have children if it's important to you, says Tracey, because time runs out. And then 'fight like hell to get back into the workforce'. She urges women to make a plan for when they'll start a family and how they'll get back into the workforce, and to engage key supporters who can help smooth the path.

What makes for a successful woman journalist?

Tracey recognised early in her career that gaining breadth of experience would be just as important to carving out a successful career as technical proficiency. She was prepared to travel and experience a range of roles across many different media, and has been able to totally reinvent her career through entering new media.

The lack of women role models in many sectors is cited as one of the key barriers to women's career success. After all, if you can't see it how can you aspire to it? Women like Mary Delahunty, Australia's first primetime solo woman news presenter, and Jana Wendt, one of the first reporters on the Australian Nine Network's version of *60 Minutes*, were trailblazers at a time when the accepted presence of women in these roles was still in its infancy. Women entering the media need to see that it can be done — you can aspire to roles that have traditionally been the sole prerogative of men. It also doesn't hurt for women to have male allies, to advocate for them and encourage them back to the workplace. After all, men still often retain the positions of power.

Jana Wendt was a particular inspiration for Tracey during her early years, and throughout her career she has had many mentors, both men and women. Today, Tracey gives back by mentoring young women through her networking group, Women in the Media.

The times, they are a-changin' for women ... aren't they?

Tracey's 'Dear Mr Sexist' letter published in *The Hoopla* took a tongue-in-cheek look at the sexist and misogynistic comments she experienced during 25 years of media.[3] It includes anecdotes about bosses commenting on her being too fat, too blonde, too wrinkly, a bit long in the tooth and in the wrong place — she should be home with the kids. These are anecdotes that may or may not be true, according to her attorney! The posting went viral, indicating there is still a lot of heat in the issue of workplace misogyny.

However, Tracey concedes that sexism and ageism were much more prevalent in the 1970s and 1980s than now. Women still have a use-by date, says Tracey, but these days it's ten or 15 years older. Today there are more job share opportunities and we are starting to see women who defy the 'fragile lollypop ladies with their skinny bodies and massive heads', as Tracey quipped in 'Dear Mr Sexist'. Tracey controversially challenged the stereotype herself when she recognised she was succumbing to the 'painted doll' image of television and published a blog showing what she looked like without makeup.[4]

Not just a women's issue

The ways in which parents must manage their work and carer responsibilities are not going to go away for employers. It's about creating flexible workplaces where mums *and* dads can share parenting, and where all employees can manage carer responsibilities, including with older parents, without jeopardising their careers. It's an issue that's relevant to everyone in the workplace.

Bob Dylan sang, 'The old road is rapidly fadin'.' Now new media and the advance of technology levels the playing field. It enables women to get back into the workplace via digital platforms, to have their columns noticed again in newspapers, and to be commentators on television and radio. The concept of women in power is starting to be normalised and workplaces are becoming more flexible, enabling employees to deliver on outcomes while also managing their carer responsibilities.

Dylan's words are starting to sound prophetic in the world of the traditional media: 'You'd better start swimming or you'll sink like a stone. For the times, they are a-changin'.'

Jennifer Keyte

Destiny's Child

Jennifer Keyte is an accomplished journalist, newsreader, presenter, MC and guest speaker. She is a 2009 Walkley Award winner.

Jennifer commenced journalism with a cadetship at radio station EON-FM in 1980, then moved on to 3XY as a reporter and wrote and read news bulletins.

In 1982 Jennifer joined Network Ten. She rapidly moved to presenting news bulletins, beginning with the early morning program *Good Morning Australia*, then regularly presenting the weekend news.

Jennifer joined the Seven Network in 1987 to co-anchor the main evening news bulletin alongside Glenn Taylor. In 1990 she became the first woman to host a primetime news bulletin solo on commercial television in Australia.

Jennifer also presented the news on the *Tonight Live* program with Steve Vizard. In 1996 she hosted *Good Medicine* and a one-off series, *Moment of Truth*, along with hosting various specials.

In 2003 Jennifer returned to the news desk at Seven Melbourne to take up the position of Weekend Newsreader. Jennifer described the move as a 'wonderful homecoming'.

In 2004 Jennifer hosted Seven's reality series *Medical Rookies*, a program that followed the country's newest doctors on their first days on the job.

Jennifer is a keen theatre-goer, a passionate Essendon supporter and enjoys travel, cycling, walking and reading. She has been involved with the Royal Children's Hospital for over 20 years and is very proud to be Patron of the Good Friday Appeal.

Jennifer has two sons — James and Alexander.

When I met Jennifer, her open face and pitch-perfect voice took me back to my early years, watching her read the six o'clock news on Channel Seven each weeknight. Our family would huddle around the television for half an hour each evening to watch the news. We were in awe of her as the first female news presenter on commercial television. The power of her presence on television today is still as strong as it ever was. What lies beneath the Keyte brand?

Igniting a passion for journalism

Jennifer has always loved children and dreamed of one day becoming a kindergarten teacher. Journalism wasn't really on her radar until she returned from a formative 'gap year', travelling with her sister across Europe and discovering the wider world beyond the leafy suburb of Essendon. Three factors began to draw her to journalism: her curiosity to debate current affairs, the recognition that she had a passion for writing, and the formative influence of a university lecturer who encouraged her writing. As Jennifer muses, destiny had found her.

The third child out of six, some of Jennifer's most vivid memories growing up in a larger family was the conversation around the dinner table with her expressive, opinionated family. Her father has a curious mind and loves a good debate. Some of Jennifer's fondest memories are of listening to talkback radio with him and discussing the issues of the day. Her mother was just as articulate and polished in her views, and was not afraid to express them.

Pushed along by the tidal wave of journalism

After work experience and a cadetship in radio (EON FM and 3XY) Jennifer was approached by Channel Ten to join their news team. Television is a collaborative sector of the media and the station decided they had enough ego-driven, big-name journalists. They were attracted to Jennifer because she was a team player. These were the heady and extravagant 1980s, when the nightly news was the jewel in the TV crown. Television had seemingly limitless budgets and journalists like Jennifer 'could do anything, be anyone'. She had some extraordinary experiences: 'I remember following Charles and Diana around Australia on their first visit when she was this very shy young girl and I was the shy young reporter.'

She covered the Ash Wednesday bushfires in 1983, proud to be part of the media, providing a true community service during a time of crisis.

In 1987, Channel Seven came knocking, offering her the chance to read the news with Glenn Taylor. This was an opportunity too good to refuse, and she relished the challenge. The work was stimulating; she loved the people, and she developed into a highly credible and popular newsreader.

Then in 1990 she was called into the General Manager's office. With some trepidation she was told the station had decided to go with only one newsreader. Her heart sank, Jennifer recalls. Then the General Manager continued: 'Yes. Glenn is leaving us.'

She was astounded. 'You mean you're going with me?' she asked.

The answer was clear: 'Yep, we think it's time for a woman on commercial television. Solo.'

Jennifer became the first solo female primetime news anchor on commercial television. She was adamant she wouldn't let her workplace down.

Being the first, one would expect Jennifer to encounter sexist remarks and innuendo in the early days of her solo role. She was certainly not immune to the casual remarks, like, 'You're a woman, you're solo, this can't last'. Yet Jennifer recalls unexpectedly brushing up against the most blatant sexist remarks, not from her colleagues, but from a visiting news director from overseas. After watching her on the news, this director said, 'Oh it's very good that you have a woman doing your news here. Very clever.'

'Why is that?' Jennifer politely asked.

'Oh, because we know women. They work harder, they don't argue back, and you don't have to pay them so much.' He laughed and thought it was hilarious. Her news director was mortified. He was looking at her, thinking, *Please, don't go psycho.*

She just said, 'Nice to meet you,' and left. She found it quite confronting that some people still thought that way. However, her style has never been one of aggression or losing her cool. While having a strong moral compass and sticking by it when it matters, she is much more comfortable treating everyone with respect and responding to situations with a calm sophistication.

The newsroom of today is very different to that of the 1970s. She says she hasn't heard such remarks in over 20 years.

Your plan, not mine

In 1995, things started to change. A new management team was appointed, bringing in their own ideas and their own people. They decided they wanted David Johnstone from Channel Ten, and made the move without consulting Jennifer.

> *'I was sitting in the makeup chair. The phone rang and the receptionist said, "Jennifer, we're getting calls from the public saying they've heard it on 3AW that David Johnstone's coming over to read the news." And I said, "What? Really? I haven't heard that." So I rang my boss upstairs and said, "Have you heard anything about this David Johnstone?" "No," he said. He denied it, denied it, denied it. I said, "Okay then, don't worry." So I got on with the job preparing for the news. Phone rang again. Receptionist again. "Jennifer, the phones are going nuts." So I rang upstairs again and I said, "You want to tell me something?" He said, "No, no, no, no, no." I thought, Righto. Sure enough, within ten minutes he rang me back. He said, "You better come upstairs."'*

She was told she would co-anchor with David Johnstone; he would kick off the show and she would follow. At that stage she was a close number two to Brian Naylor, the number one newsreader in Melbourne at the time, for Channel Nine.

> *'I wondered — if they were going to bring someone in to read with*

> *Brian Naylor, would they discuss it with him or would he hear it from the radio? Or do you actually discuss it with your main anchor? And that's what hurt — that they didn't consult me.'*

Her contract was coming up for renewal, so she told them she needed to think about what she wanted to do next. They were horrified. 'Oh no, you have to stay. You have to sign. This is our big plan,' they said. She replied, 'It might be your big plan. Doesn't mean it's mine.'

She had been incredibly loyal to Channel Seven and loved the news team, so this decision was like a kick in the guts. But it was also a wake-up call — you can be too naïve at times, she reflects. She was heartbroken as Channel Seven had been like a second family to her, but there was no going back.

Seeking her own path

Jennifer didn't have another work offer, so leaving took great courage. It was the first time she'd been on her own and it was like stepping off a cliff, she recalls. This was her first big crash and she needed time to heal.

After taking a holiday with her sister she decided not to rush into the next job, and spent time meeting with prospective employers, listening to offers. None of them really sparked her interest.

Career choices are a bit like being in a room with multiple doors — which one do you open? Jennifer needed help to make that decision. That help came when she met Isaac Apel, a commercial advisor who took her under his wing. 'He is the reason for my success,' she says with pride.

Isaac sourced and negotiated the next role for her at Channel Nine, at that stage the market leader and flush with funds. It was a great opportunity for Jennifer to find her own path and reinvent herself. She accepted the offer on the condition that she would not compete with the Channel Seven news team.

She worked across a range of shows, including presenting the medical show *Good Medicine*, reading the news from Sydney, and helping out on the *Today Show* and other morning shows. This experience helped shape her identity, test her limits and stretch her capability.

Falling in love with motherhood

Thinking back to the 1980s, Jennifer recalls looking around the newsroom and noticing that all the fabulous women she worked with fell into one of two categories: either they didn't have children, or they fell pregnant and left. She remembers, 'Every time a woman got pregnant we had a cake, we said goodbye and we never saw her again.' Most of the men in the newsroom were parents, but with a wife at home to look after the children and the house, those men could work the hours and undertake the travel that news demands. It was frustrating to see these talented women being lost to the station.

Nowadays there are systems in place, such as job sharing, so a lot of women reporters have children. However, it is still a challenge keeping all the balls in the air. Media can be a brutal and all-consuming profession for men as well as women. There comes a stage, especially for women, when they need to make choices about family before they lose themselves totally in the profession. This stage came for Jennifer in her late thirties, when she felt her biological clock was heading towards midnight and her opportunity to become pregnant was closing. Jennifer always assumed she would be a mother, so not having children was never an option for her.

The happiest time of her life was when she found out she was pregnant. And then it was absolutely joyous when both her boys were born, two and a half years apart. Of course, it was hard work — particularly the banal, mind-numbing drudgery of the day-to-day. But her feelings of motherhood were intensely passionate and she surrendered herself to them, savouring every single moment — and still does. Motherhood is the most important job of her life. At the same time her passion for keeping her career on track was as strong as ever.

Channel Nine was highly supportive of Jennifer's return to part-time work after maternity leave. Although Jennifer didn't mention this, I reflected that it would have helped that she had such a strong presence and was much loved by the viewers.

Returning to work when she had two small children meant running the household with military precision. Jennifer says she has found a new level of appreciation for her mother, who brought up six children while also managing to carve out a career for herself. She remembers some very practical and helpful advice from her mother, along the lines of: 'As a grandmother, I'm happy to babysit and help you with whatever you need, but I'm not your nanny.' She was thankful for her mother's honesty and for setting these boundaries, which enabled her to get on with organising the practical support she needed. One of the best things she did was to hire a highly capable nanny, who remains with the family today.

Back where she belongs

While she loved her job and was devoted to her career, with motherhood came a reluctance to continue the punishing travel schedules her Sydney roles demanded. Another change of management, this time at Channel Seven, led to an offer to return to a Melbourne-based role. This was like a siren call to Jennifer, as her heart had always been with Channel Seven, but there was a catch — she was still under contract with Channel Nine. Nine had looked after her, so her loyalties were divided, but they were unable to offer her significant opportunities in Melbourne.

Then things got ugly. Despite Isaac's best efforts, the decision-makers at Channel Nine were not prepared to release her. Lawyers got involved and threats of injunctions were thrown around. Jennifer decided it was time for her to take a personal role and cut through the legal wrangling. She personally rang Channel Nine's CEO, and persuaded him to release her from the contract, on the basis that they couldn't offer her anything substantial in Melbourne. He respected her for her honesty and integrity in making the call, and after thinking it over he agreed to release her from her contract.

Stepping back into the newsroom for the weekend news at Channel Seven felt right. She recalls being overwhelmed when, at the conclusion of her first bulletin, the news crew unfurled streamers and cheered her return. She realised then that she had come home.

Part of Jennifer's life now includes sharing her insights with other young women embarking on a career in media. I asked her about the main issues concerning these women, and how she mentors them about finding that elusive balance between maintaining a challenging and stimulating career, and being a loving and successful parent.

The decision to start a family

Jennifer urges women to start a family when the time is right for them, rather than waiting for the perfect moment to step off the career track. The perfect moment may never come, and you may delay the decision only to miss the opportunity altogether. 'Have them younger, as it doesn't get easier,' says Jennifer. 'Do whatever it takes,' is her advice to women starting a family.

She reflects on an incident when an IVF specialist working on *Good Medicine* came into the office one day when they were all working frantically, thumped the desk and said:

> *'Will you women hurry up and have your children. I'm so tired of trying to make all these old women have kids. Get on with it. Put me out of business, please. The heartache, the challenges, the money, the emotional cost, the physical cost of what I'm doing to older women is killing me.'*

Success is where preparation meets opportunity

Today's newsroom is very different to that of the 1970s — women are no longer the exception that warrants the same level of smart comments or innuendo. For Jennifer, 'success is where preparation meets opportunity'. Be a stand-out professional from the start of your career. The quality of your preparation and research means your work will speak for itself. Be open to opportunities, experiencing different organisations and jobs, and reinvent yourself at critical career points. I would add: when you are a top-performing employee, you will have earned some flexibility when you need it as a new parent.

Be true to yourself

Just as importantly, live an authentic life. Research and report the news in your way and in your style, and push back if you're asked to cross your own boundaries. Jennifer recalls that in the early days of journalism she would be asked to knock on the door and seek interviews with families whose child had died — if they didn't want to talk, she respected that and left them alone. When criticised back at the station for not pushing the family to get the story, she would reply: 'That's not me. If you want someone to do that, send another journalist.'

Find advocates

Having powerful role models and mentors in the workplace is critical. Jana Wendt took Jennifer under her wing. Jennifer also looked up to Annette Allison, a Ten News anchor. Isaac has been invaluable in promoting Jennifer's career. Strong mentors will have an eye for opportunities and will advocate for you in places inaccessible to you.

Recognise that media can be tough for everyone

Jennifer describes media as a tough, brutal and confronting sector, for all involved. Men can get treated appallingly, too, and it takes a good measure of resilience for anyone to work through the ruthlessness of the sector. She recalls attending what was known as a 'reptiles lunch' in Sydney, where executives would bring in journalists and give them a 'total roast' for entertainment. It may have been funny for the executives, but it was tough for the journos. Jennifer remembers thinking it was like the old gladiator days. That kind of message gets sent down the line about what's acceptable behaviour. But then you have the opportunity to work for a decent man and fantastic boss like Kerry Stokes, says Jennifer, and you realise it doesn't have to be that way. You have the choice whether to participate in this type of behaviour or not, and whether to work for that kind of employer or move on.

Achieving the balance

It seems Jennifer has successfully navigated the difficult journey through career and parenthood one step at a time, and now leads a very full life that includes both a rewarding career and a happy family. She considers herself very fortunate not to have experienced the hostility she knows other women have had to confront when attempting to combine a career and motherhood. On reflection, I would conclude that it's not through good fortune that Jennifer has escaped the ruthlessness of the tough media culture, but rather that her moral compass has guided her decisions and enabled her to achieve what she wants in life, without compromising her integrity.

Lucinda Dunn, OAM

Dancing to Her Own Beat

Lucinda Dunn, OAM, received her early training in Sydney with Janece Graham and Tanya Pearson, before going on to win a Prix de Lausanne scholarship to study at the Royal Ballet School, London. While in London she also performed with Birmingham Royal Ballet. In 1991 Lucinda joined the Australian Ballet Company, and was promoted to principal artist in 2002. She has also been awarded several scholarships to study overseas and has been partnered by many international guests of the Australian Ballet. A diverse and musical dancer with a strong technique, Lucinda excels in the pure classical ballets and enjoys portraying characters in story ballets, as well as the physicality of contemporary pieces. Lucinda has been a guest of the Royal Danish Ballet, Jeunne Ballet de France, a Principal guest of the Birmingham Royal Ballet, and been invited to perform in prestigious International Ballet Festivals. Lucinda is Australia's Longest Serving Ballerina, retiring in 2014. In January 2015 she was appointed Artistic Director of the Tanya Pearson Classical Coaching Academy.

Lucinda Dunn takes us into her world of whirlwind tours, international accolades, punishing work schedules, having babies and performing onstage after sleepless nights. She tells her story with the thoughtful and calm assurance of someone who applies tough discipline to everything she does, tempered with a relaxed confidence.

Preparation, coupled with an extraordinary work ethic, has been the hallmark of Lucinda's success. Yet there is another theme that has guided her in all her steps, and that is about family. Her life pirouettes around her multiple roles of devoted daughter, dedicated mother, loving wife and proud sister, prima ballerina and budding director of a ballet academy. Somehow she has succeeded at them all, and has carved out a happy, successful and fulfilling life. But not every day was bright and sunny. There were times when it took all her physical and emotional reserves, her fierce determination and an unwavering strength of character to make it through.

'I didn't come out of the womb in splits'

I was shocked. It was quite extraordinary for one of the Australian Ballet's greatest principal dancers in recent times to say she'd hoped to sing in musicals over dancing en-pointe when she was a child. I expected her to be one of those young girls watching *Swan Lake* and telling her mum she wanted to dance as Odette when she grew up. Singing, acting and dancing are, however, in her blood. Her father was a stage director and carpenter, constructing stage scenery, and her mother was a child actress, working in West End musicals in London, and later on board cruise ships. They fell in love with each other and with Australia, immigrating to Sydney before starting a family; Lucinda was born first, then her brother two years later.

Lucinda talks of an idyllic childhood, but not an easy one for her mother. Her father died when she was three years old and her mother never remarried. Lucinda and her brother had all the love and support they could have possibly wanted, but lived on a shoestring budget. Her mother made ends meet by teaching in a local dance school, and numerous other jobs. School holidays meant camping in their tiny caravan at caravan parks with friends, and simply enjoying their time together.

Lucinda's earliest memories were of being onstage, just like her mother, which was exactly where she wanted to be. By age four she was tap-dancing, by the time she was five she was dancing jazz and ballet. She loved singing and dancing in musicals, and ballet was far from her mind back then. She recalls her first television appearance, when Channel Seven interviewed some aspiring young dancers in her school during a tour from London's Royal Ballet. All the young dancers said they wanted to be ballerinas. Then Lucinda piped up, all braces and bright eyes, and said quite firmly: 'I want to be in musicals.'

Her entrée to ballet

Lucinda first met Tanya Pearson at age 13, when the Tanya Pearson Classical Coaching Academy and her local ballet school merged premises. Mrs Pearson saw something in Lucinda and predicted she would become a ballet dancer. She followed that hunch and offered Lucinda the opportunity to join her prestigious European tour. This is where she became exposed to the heady and exciting international world of ballet academies and competitions. She entered the Prix de Lausanne and out of hundreds that auditioned was the only Australian to proceed to the finals. From there she was offered a scholarship to almost any ballet school in the world. No longer as passionate about singing in musicals, she decided she would give ballet a go and see where it might lead. She left high school for the Royal Ballet School in London. Her mum and younger brother relocated to England to support her, and so her entrée into the international world of ballet had begun. She had no idea that this decision would change her life irrevocably.

Within a few months of accepting the scholarship, however, she began experiencing severe back pain and was horrified to hear she had been diagnosed with a serious stress fracture. She was placed in a plaster cast from her hipbones to her armpits, for '12 weeks and three hours' or 121,140 minutes. Whichever way you calculate it, the time must have seemed endless to the 15-year-old Lucinda. It must have been painful to watch her friends dance in the studio of the prestigious Royal Ballet School while she sat on the sidelines not being able to dance a step. When you're young, you think you're strong, invincible and can do anything. Lucinda learned a hard lesson at a very young age: her body was vulnerable to injury, and injury would always be part of a dancer's life.

She returned to Australia at the end of the year and experienced a full recovery, then went back to the Royal Ballet School the following year to complete her scholarship. This is when she thrived, dancing with the Birmingham Royal Ballet Company for three months.

Then Maina Gielgud AO, Artistic Director for the Australian Ballet at the time, saw her talent and potential to excel at dance, and invited her to return to Australia and join her company. Here was another critical decision point: as a young 17-year-old, bright-eyed and enthusiastic, should she continue dancing on the international stage or return to Melbourne? She missed her family terribly and was motivated by the prospect of working for the inspiring Maina Gielgud, but her decision was a difficult one, as a contract to join the Birmingham Royal Ballet was also very appealing. After some time she had made a decision. It was 3am Sydney time, but she couldn't wait until the morning. She was on the phone to her mum with the words: 'Mum, I'm coming home.'

Ten years of growth

Lucinda joined the Australian Ballet in 1991, and flourished under Maina Gielgud's technical training, mentorship and nurturing. Looking back over her career, Lucinda recognises that she has always been motivated by an exceptionally robust work ethic: 'I was a really hard worker in the studio and I really believe the saying, "The more sweat I shed in practice, the less blood in battle".'

Lucinda put herself through a grueling work schedule, including long days in the studio, and many weeks each year extensively touring Australia. One can see Maina's influence here, a great believer that success comes from a huge amount of preparation in the studio, in rehearsal and at home. This preparation then sets you free, says Maina, to interpret the work your way.[1]

This was a formative decade. Within ten years Lucinda had developed an impressive reputation, and rose to Principal Artist by 2002. In the late 1990s, she met Danilo Radojevic, a retired star dancer himself, with an illustrious career in the American Ballet Theatre. He was then a ballet master brought over from the US by the Artistic Director at the time, Ross Stretton. Danilo and Lucinda were married in 2001.

Good timing

Prior to 2007, women dancers who were considering starting a family had to make one of two choices: either give up a successful dancing career or remain childless. Many women dancers are at their peak artistically and emotionally in the critical childbearing years of their 20s to 30s, and it is often a painful choice to make. At that time there were no support systems in place during pregnancy or after the birth, and it was simply expected that dancers would give up their successful careers once they became pregnant. David McAllister, the ballet's Artistic Director, recognised the enormous talent drain of female dancers leaving in the peak of their careers and decided to do something about it. In 2007, he introduced the safe work duties policy. Under this policy, women who became pregnant were not assumed to resign; instead, they were offered non-dancing roles behind the scenes in areas of their interest until they were physically and emotionally ready to return to the stage. It made perfect sense in hindsight, yet it took a leader with vision to conceive of it and make it a reality.

This approach immediately transformed the career prospects of ballerinas, and has been utilised by at least ten female dancers since its inception. The introduction of this policy was timed perfectly for Lucinda and Danilo. In 2008, Lucinda was in her mid-thirties, at the height of her physical strength and dancing career. She realised starting a family had to happen soon, and luckily she became pregnant with Claudia.

While she loved being a mum, she was committed to returning to the ballet. She knew that with dedication and preparation, she hoped she could return to her peak performance and continue dancing in her prime for several years. So, only five months after giving birth, she was back onstage in a white unitard!

Coming back to work had multiple benefits. For one, it gave her access to the Pilates studio and physiotherapy advice, thereby enabling her to return to peak performance in record time. Just as importantly, pre-birth she took advantage of the safe work policy, working in a range of back-of-house functions, including working with the wardrobe department, with costumes and with the philanthropy team. She took reception calls on the front desk and sold merchandise. She coached dancers in the studio and taught ballet classes. She put one ballet onstage. Being exposed to such a variety of roles helped her understand and appreciate the behind-the-scenes business processes that make the ballet such a success. The additional skills she learned along the way also prepared her for the next stage of her career after retiring from dancing.

Ballet, baby and me

Keeping physically fit, staying en pointe and having babies was always going to be a juggle. Yet it never occurred to Lucinda that she could fail to deliver on all three. She continued to dance the 'Dance of the Sugar Plum Fairy' in *The Nutcracker* eight weeks into her pregnancy with Claudia, although she reflects: 'That role killed me, full stop. Let alone when you've got no stamina, feel sick and dizzy.'[2] She also took classes up to the day before Claudia was born. 'I loved being in lycra with belly and boobs, and I just felt that it was part of me.' The second time around, with Ava, she continued dancing until 13 weeks, in *Checkmate*.

Family had always been front and centre of Lucinda's life, and was more important now than ever. She decided to become actively involved in parenting, to be there for her babies as much as possible, with support from a nanny when necessary. Fortunately, she was able to take both the babies to work with her and was able to breastfeed while at work. Her mother and mother-in-law were available during the day and at critical times, travelling to her home base of Melbourne at times.

Danilo loved being a father. Parenting duties were a genuine 50/50 split between the two of them. Touring together with her husband and the babies was great fun, though it required a lot of organisation, Lucinda recalls. She was so fortunate to be married to someone who could always be by her side.

Raising the barre

Lucinda's greatest strengths — her tremendous work ethic and drive for perfection — had a dark side. Despite the outstanding reviews and accolades, and the standing ovations as the curtain falls each night, Lucinda acknowledges she has always been her own worst critic. Even at her peak, she recalls,

> *'There would only be a handful of times out of thousands and thousands of performances where I went home satisfied that that was the best I could do, where I would say, "I worked really hard for that. Everything I hoped for came to fruition. I pulled off what I thought I could and I enjoyed it and I told a story."'*

This determination to be the best, coupled with her relentless self-criticism, may be manageable when you're single and dancing is your whole life, but it comes at a price when combined with marriage and motherhood. Dancing is a very self-indulgent career, requiring 100 percent commitment, Lucinda confesses. So when it came to accommodating motherhood, life wasn't always easy. She experienced the best and worst of emotions around motherhood guilt, exhaustion, sleepless nights and questioning herself, while determinedly focusing on returning to peak performance. When returning to work after having Claudia, Lucinda recalls,

> *'I was exhausted. I was pushing my body uphill every day, then going home to a baby who wouldn't sleep for more than small increments at a time. I just remember sitting under the barre one day and thinking: "Someone else is at the park with my baby and I'm sitting in this studio, feeling exhausted, depressed, can't dance, don't want to dance. What am I doing?" I just wanted to be with my baby. I remember the guilt about handing my baby over and then her crying, wanting me as I left the door. I'd be crying, the baby would be crying, then Mum would call me before I'd even turned on the ignition in the car and say, "She's fine."'*

So what kept Lucinda going? Why continue to push herself through a punishing work schedule, enduring relentless exhaustion after days, weeks and months of sleepless nights? Lucinda isn't really sure — she just hoped every night would be a bit better, plus her passion for dancing kept her motivated. 'You want to push yourself every day and better yourself every day,' she reflects. 'If you don't have that passion and enjoyment it's too hard to go on.' However, she recognises that without the practical and emotional support of her mother, mother-in-law and husband, she couldn't have made it through on her own.

In 2012, six months after giving birth to her second child, Ava, she went on tour with the Australian Ballet to New York, dancing in Graham Murphy's *Swan Lake*. She had pushed herself to her physical and emotional limits preparing for this tour, placing enormous expectations on herself. She was jet-lagged and exhausted. On top of it all, every minute of the day she was thinking of her girls and how long it would be before she'd return home and be able to hold them again. On opening night, she received flowers in her dressing room with a card saying, 'Mummy, please dance for us.' The flowers and card were, of course, from Claudia and Ava. That was almost too much torment. She broke down, devastated her girls couldn't be with her, and instructed Danilo to take the flowers out of the room or she wouldn't be able to compose herself.

Then, at the end of the performance: 'I remember almost collapsing on a swan in the wings at the end of the ballet and just heaving; the fact that I'd done it, I felt a massive relief that I had got through the performance at all,' she recalls.

Dancing is 50 percent physical and 50 percent mental strength, says Lucinda. That was never truer than in New York. Needless to say, the New York tour was a resounding success and the production received standing ovations.

The pirouette

Lucinda holds the record for the longest-serving female principal Ballerina in Australia, retiring just after turning 40.

There comes a time in every dancer's life when injury becomes too much, and towards the end of her career Lucinda was experiencing repeated injuries. Nicole Sharp, Tanya Pearson's daughter, approached her to take over as Artistic Director of the Tanya Pearson Classical Coaching Academy when she was ready to leave the stage. Although this was an offer she would have previously rejected out of hand, she now started to take it seriously. Lucinda had physically struggled so much in the final months of dancing that it was somewhat of a relief to let go and transition to an alternative career. Having worked across a range of roles in the Australian Ballet, she had confidence that she could learn how to successfully direct a prestigious ballet academy.

Lucinda had come full circle, stepping off the stage in retirement to return to her starting position at the Academy.

It's early days yet, having taken over the school in January 2015, however coaching and teaching seems like the logical next step for her. Being Director at the Academy enables her to express her love of dancing and fulfils her desire to pass on her skills, experience and insights to budding dancers. Prior to taking up this role she spent several wonderful months with her children, appreciating the ordinary moments of being a mother: making the school and kindy drop-offs, heading to the supermarket at midday and having space during the weekend to hang out with Danilo and the girls. Now that Danilo has retired from the dancing world, he is also relishing spending more time with the girls, living in Manly and helping take the pressure off Lucinda when she works.

Ballet class

Lucinda is passionate about teaching strong technique, instilling a strong work ethic and providing the foundations to enable dancers to be the best they can be. She is placing her own stamp on the Academy now, applying the lessons that were important to her when she was developing as an artist. However, passing on thc lcssons one learns in life are just as important as teaching ballet class. I asked Lucinda what she would say if she could advise her younger self, using the knowledge she has now. She would impart the following wisdom:

- Don't be in a rush to return to work early after having a child. Cherish time with your baby. I may have driven myself to go back too soon — certainly I don't remember it as being a happy time. Trying to be a successful new mum is exhausting; don't underestimate it.
- Accept that mother guilt is a hard thing to deal with. Being passionate about your work, and having a deep desire to continue and to improve yourself every day will alleviate your guilt, but it will always be there. That's okay.
- Surround yourself with great supporters. Seek out a strong mentor who can teach you, sponsor you and advocate on your behalf, find a wonderful partner, and appreciate your parents and friends who are there to help. I chose to hire a nanny to be there while I was working, and be a hands-on mum as soon as I walked through the front door. That worked for me. Find out what works for you.

- Know when it's time to hang up your ballet shoes and listen to that inner voice that tells you it's enough. I left at the right time — if I had retired earlier when I was still strong and secure with my place in the ballet world, it may have been too soon. But don't be one of those dancers who pushes themselves too far, are forced off the stage through injury or have the audience tell you it's enough and time to go.
- Finally, the most important lesson I can teach you is to learn to do things for yourself. To aim for self satisfaction. Don't try to impress other people. You'll want to impress them at the start of your dancing career, and it may be important for a time, but ultimately be true to yourself. Interpret the dance your way and you'll find your own rhythm.

Dr Sharon Lierse

Single White Female

Dr Sharon Lierse is currently Lecturer in the School of Education at Charles Darwin University, Melbourne campus. She is leading the development and consolidation of research and professional experience for educators at the newly formed campus.

Prior to her appointment at Charles Darwin University, she was Associate Professor in the Faculty of Music and Performing Arts at Universiti Pendidikan Sultan Idris in Malaysia. Here she set up an orchestral program, developed a research seminar series for post-graduate students and was founder and Managing Editor of the Malaysian Music Journal (MMJ).

Dr Lierse has also lectured in tertiary learning and teaching at the University of Tasmania, and has been the Manager of Professional Learning at the Australian Council for Educational Research. She has also had extensive experience as an educator in schools.

Dr Lierse has been an active researcher and has presented papers in every state of Australia, Asia, the United Kingdom, Europe, the United States, Canada and Brazil. As a performer, she has toured Australia, Asia and Europe as a soloist and chamber musician. Her research interests encompass the performing arts in education, arts education in Asia, curriculum and assessment, and excellence in teaching.

Sharon's quest for a successful career in music has taken many twists and turns, some planned, some totally unexpected. Along the way her passion for teaching, her talent for music and her ability to succeed have been tested to the full. She has had to create her own portfolio, and has grasped opportunities as they became available throughout Australia and overseas, across social and organisational cultures. She has known the shock of discovering that her hard-won music practice was not going to sustain her academic ambitions, having to close her highly successful practice at short notice and take a leap into the unknown.

Facing the music

Music is at the core of Sharon Lierse's life. Teaching and music have always been Sharon's lifelong passions, and she has worked unrelentingly to combine both into a successful career. It's not surprising, given she came from a musical family — her mother, Anne Lierse, was Director of Music at Melbourne High School and still teaches in a private studio, and her brother plays in the Melbourne Symphony Orchestra. She was brought up with music from her earliest years. She started teaching music at the tender age of 16, specialising in cello, flute, double bass and theory.

Always academically focused, Sharon completed a Bachelor of Music from the Conservatorium at the University of Melbourne, followed by a Social Sciences Degree with Honours at La Trobe University. She added to these a Graduate Diploma in Education from the University of Melbourne and a Post-graduate Diploma in Management Studies from the Melbourne Business School. Her desire to move into academia led to the completion of a PhD over a seven-year period, finishing in 2005. Tenured jobs in education were very hard to come by at this time. Sharon remembers applying for around 100 lecturing jobs (she still has the applications on her computer) and was frequently provided with the same worn-out reasons for not getting a job — she was overqualified, though lacked experience as a lecturer.

'This is the chicken or the egg; if you can't get experience as a lecturer then you can't get a lecturing position,' she recalls. It took Sharon many years to gain a permanent role, and then it was only for one day per week.

One day she was discussing her career frustrations over lunch with a respected professor. He gave her some perceptive advice that shook her world — she needed to work overseas for a year or two to gain the credentials for an academic career in Australia. This would mean giving up her reputable, hard-won private practice, which had grown to around 50 students and had supported her financially during her PhD. It also meant leaving her family and friends and taking a chance on a fixed-term position overseas, with no guarantee of employment when she returned to Australia.

From the romance of Vienna to the harsh reality of the Malaysian jungle

Reluctantly, Sharon realised she needed to follow this advice. She started applying for overseas lecturing positions. Ideally, as a musician she preferred to gain experience in Europe — specifically Vienna, Switzerland or Germany. Nevertheless, she applied for every suitable overseas posting, including one at a remote and obscure university in Malaysia that she had never heard of, 80 kilometres north of Kuala Lumpur in the state of Perak. Here's what happened next, as Sharon recalls it:

> *'A few weeks later I received an email from them saying, "We don't have your passport, you didn't send in your passport copy." I thought that was a very odd question, so I asked them, "So where am I in the selection process?" and they said, "Oh, we've offered you the job." So that was a bit strange. They hadn't even met me.'*

Three weeks later she was on a plane to Malaysia, with only 20 kilograms of luggage, to take up a role as Senior Lecturer at the Universiti Pendidikan Sultan Idris (UPSI). She packed up her practice, found alternative teachers for all her students, sold her car, received her visa, organised her personal finances, finalised accommodation in Malaysia and arranged her travel — in record time. She had gone over for a quick reconnoitre a few weeks earlier, and had rented out a small, barely furnished student apartment. What else was there to do?

UPSI offers undergraduate and postgraduate programs in teacher training. According to its website, the state of Perak is renowned for its ageless architectural splendour and holiday getaways. But it's no big city like Kuala Lumpur, and the expatriate experience is somewhat more humble than the exotic life offered in a big city. Even at the time Sharon attended, lectures were taught in English, which made it easier for her. The local language, Bahasa Malay, was the first language spoken by everyone, so Sharon did pick it up while she was there.

Sharon arrived on the first day of Ramadan and began teaching the next day — knowing no-one, without speaking the language, with minimal knowledge of the local Islamic culture, without a car and staying in very basic student accommodation. But she was ready for the experience, and looks back on it as a great period of learning.

The first Australian

UPSI is an Islamic, government-run university. Most students are Malay and observe all Islamic traditions, including the five daily prayers, fasting during the month of Ramadan, and observe a multitude of other religious celebrations. The university's schedule is planned around these activities and events.

In the early days, Sharon was intrigued by the triplication of things. In her apartment block she noticed three 7-Eleven stores adjacent to each other — one was owned by a Malay person, one by a Chinese Malaysian person and one by a Tamil Indian person. There were three places of worship in town, locals observed three sets of public holidays and religious feast days throughout the year, including Chinese New Year, Ramadan, Thaipusan and Christmas, to name a few, and practiced three different sets of cultural values, beliefs and behaviours. Sharon soon realised the importance religion played in the cultural life of the community, and the different levels of integration of these cultures.

UPSI employs many international lecturers and teachers, largely from Indonesia, the Middle East, India or Africa, plus a handful of Western lecturers. Sharon was the first Australian. By comparison to Australia's way of life, Sharon felt rural Malaysia was far from a paradise, though Malaysia did have a unique grandeur of its own, with its prehistoric rainforests, mountains, caves and beaches.

Worlds collide

One of the things Sharon missed most about Australia was the relative personal freedom, such as dressing how she liked, travelling how she chose, behaving how she wanted (within reason) and expressing herself freely. Within a few days of arrival, it became clear that she needed to make some important personal decisions about these matters.

First, she needed to decide whether to conform to the tradition of wearing a hijab (a headscarf that covers the hair, ears and neck). Although there was no legal pressure to wear a hijab in Malaysia, there was strong peer pressure at the university and in the community to conform. For pragmatic reasons, Sharon chose to follow the local custom — she wore a baju kurung (a traditional Malay outfit) and wore her long hair up in a comb. It enabled her to blend in to some extent, and avoid some of the stares and comments of men in public, which she experienced on a daily basis.

Secondly, Sharon needed to make a decision about how to travel around. After observing the erratic driving habits of the locals Sharon decided to walk, use the local bus or take taxis rather than drive. It was during these walks and bus trips that Sharon discovered another cultural subtlety — women were always in groups; they shared apartments, shopped together and ate in restaurants together. Also, single women were chaperoned until they were married.

Now things started to make sense for her — she began to understand why men persisted in asking about her age, marital status and children. Being a single white female was a curiosity to some locals, which was amusing to Sharon sometimes. But at other times she felt like a target for men, who hassled her in the street and displayed ugly attitudes towards her as a single woman. She discovered that single women in the traditional Malay Muslim society were generally viewed in two ways: as either marriage prospects or as immoral. She stood out as a female living alone, walking unaccompanied and eating in local cafés by herself — in effect breaking one of the most significant social norms for women in the community. Being an open, outgoing and fun-loving person, Sharon had to learn to curb her friendliness and keep her private life to herself.

She quickly lost patience with the assumptions around her integrity and the intrusive questioning by others. She sought the advice of other expatriate women and discovered they had resolved this problem simply by constructing a culturally acceptable story. So she practised some standard, satisfactory responses to questions, and discovered it worked for her. These included:

Question: What is your name?
Answer: (make up a name)
Question: How old are you?
Answer: 28.
Question: Where are you from?
Answer: Australia.
Question: Are you married?
Answer: Yes.
Question: Do you have children?
Answer: No, I've only been married for one year.
Question: Where is your husband?
Answer: On the way, visa issues.

Asking tradesmen to come to the apartment was always an interesting experience. Living alone meant she was unable to invite a man into her apartment or have him come in while she was away, so was forced to take a day off work, remain at the apartment and leave the door wide open when a lock needed to be fixed, or an electrician or plumber was needed. She remembers the men's embarrassment at going into the apartment of a single woman, and the way they nervously scurried off without even accepting a glass of water from her. Of course, it was impossible for her to invite any male friend or colleague to her apartment — that would have totally destroyed her reputation among the more conservative of the locals.

A foot in both worlds

As Sharon discovered, Malaysia can be a difficult place in which to mix with the local community, especially if you are female, single and without children. It's easier to make expatriate friends rather than local friends, and the expatriate clubs and embassies are the safest and easiest places in which to socialise.

Despite these restrictions, Sharon made substantial inroads in getting to know her students and being accepted, to the extent possible, as a foreigner. Although never having been invited into their homes except for formal faculty events, towards the end of her tenure she felt tremendously honoured to be invited to a Malaysian wedding as the only non-Malaysian guest.

Perhaps this closeness came about because of her respectful approach to the students and the sensitivity she displayed toward their religious and cultural differences. No doubt becoming culturally self-aware gave her a unique insight into the effect her behaviour had on others, and gave her the edge over some expatriate lecturers.

Much of Western classical music, including opera, has its roots in the Christian religion — composers such as Bach and Handel wrote music specifically for the Lutheran Church. As Western music was considered immoral in Malaysia, it was no surprise that students had no exposure to it. Sharon had to tread carefully around the dilemma of how to teach religious music in an inoffensive way. She decided to neutralise the names of some of the pieces — for instance, she changed the *Christmas Concerto* to the *Corelli Concerto No. 8 in G Major*, so students would not be offended by being asked to play Christian music.

She recalls another instance where she was lecturing on Western music, a subject most students disliked because they couldn't relate to it. It was mid-afternoon during the month of Ramadan, when the students were fasting and half the students were falling asleep through lack of food. She had to think creatively about how to engage them, enhance their learning and have some fun along the way:

> *'I put on a recording of Handel's* Messiah, *and we got to the "Hallelujah" chorus. I began to sing along with it, with all the entries, singing, "He shall reign." I was having fun, and they were looking at me with these big saucer eyes, like I'd gone crazy. At the end there was just stony silence. And I said, "Put up your hand if you've ever heard it." No-one did. They did, however, comment that the music was beautiful.'*

This approach paid off. At the end of her tenure she received top scores in student evaluations — the only lecturer to receive such high ratings.

What is culture?

'A nation's culture resides in the hearts and in the soul of its people.'
— Mahatma Gandhi

A country's culture is the context through which citizens construct their world. It comprises the beliefs, norms, values and behaviour practised by people. It is often unconscious until, like Sharon, we travel and experience a culture clash.

Professor Geert Hofstede is credited as the founder of comparative intercultural research. Hofstede defines culture as 'a collective programming of the mind which distinguishes the members of one category of people from another'.[1] His six-dimensional model of national cultures shifted the paradigm in which cultural integration and difference is now understood. It would be useful to reflect on this model momentarily, to contrast cultures across Australian and Malaysian societies. The differences are shown below.

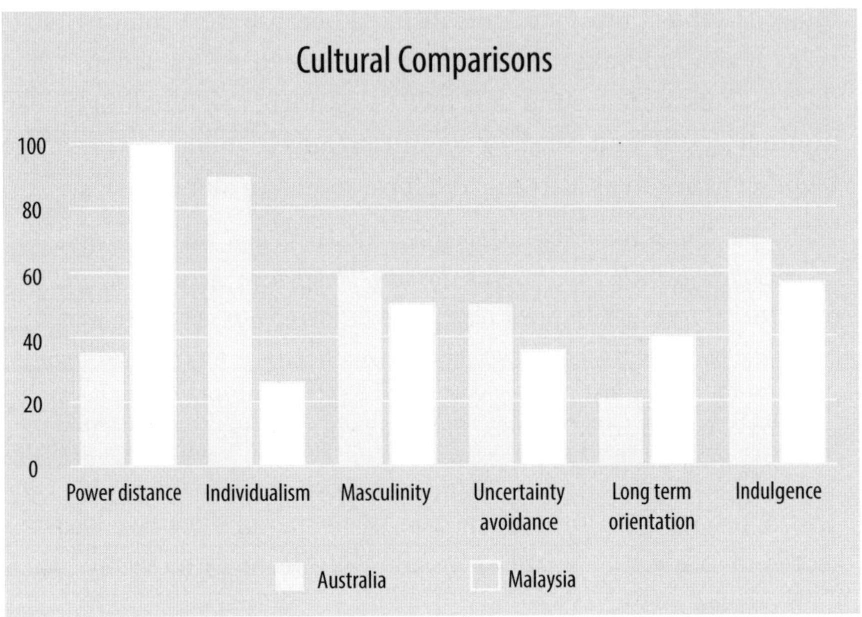

Under his framework, there are two cultural dimensions that are particularly at odds when comparing these cultures: power distance and individualism. What do they mean and how did these differences play out in daily life for Sharon?

Power distance[2]

Malaysian people have the highest power distance score in the world. This means they tend to accept hierarchy in an organisation as essentially inequitable, are comfortable with the centralisation of power, subordinates expect to be told what to do, and the ideal boss is a benevolent autocrat. In the workplace, communication tends to be formal and challenges to leadership are not well received.

Australia's low power distance score, on the other hand, suggests that hierarchy in our culture is viewed more as a matter of convenience. Australians expect superiors to be always accessible, managers and employees expect to be consulted and information is shared frequently. Communication tends to be informal, direct and participative.

When looked at through the Hofstede lens, the power distance dimension played out at UPSI in a number of ways, most obviously with students refusing to put up their hand to ask questions, to participate in discussions or challenge lecturers. It took all of Sharon's creative nous to encourage students to participate in class or in music practice.

Sharon also observed power distance at work around access to senior staff. For instance, to see the Vice Chancellor, Sharon had to run the gauntlet of three inner sanctums, all fiercely guarded by a clutch of executive assistants. In contrast, in Australia it would not be all that unusual to bail up a Vice Chancellor in the corridor of some universities for a chat.

Power distance also influenced social behaviour in routine day-to-day interactions. Sharon was on a bus one day that broke down and she got off, as any Australian would. Then she turned around and saw a Malaysian girl sitting glued to her seat in the bus, waiting for the driver to give her permission to disembark.

At times, this power distance worked to Sharon's advantage. If she was being ignored, given poor service or waiting at the end of a long line, she simply needed to introduce herself as Professor Mudya Doctor Sharon, and she would immediately get the attention she needed — behaviour she wouldn't dare try on back in Australia! Phone not working? Just mention your title of Professor or Doctor, and you'll get it attended to immediately. At the airport her title would quickly get her through the diplomatic zone.

Individualism[3]

Malaysia is a collectivistic society, meaning there is a close, long-term commitment to the group in which you belong, be that a family, extended family or extended relationships. Loyalty is paramount and overrides most other societal rules and regulations. This type of society fosters strong relationships, where each person takes responsibility for fellow members of their group. In collectivistic societies, offence leads to shame and loss of face.

By contrast, Australia is a highly individualistic culture. It's a loosely knit society in which people are expected to look after themselves and their immediate families. In the business world, employees are expected to be self-reliant and display initiative. Hiring and promotion decisions are based on merit or evidence of achievement.

The sense of collectivism in Malaysia in part explains the social norm of women not being seen alone in public. It may also explain the logistics of chaperoning women in Malaysia. Sharon recalls organising a scholarship for a Malaysian student to attend a music conference in Australia. Sharon observed that many students hadn't applied to attend such conferences, and couldn't understand why the chosen female student was reluctant to attend this high-profile event. Then it struck her.

> *'I went through the whole planning process in great detail; at the end she looked at me strangely and said, "But who's going to chaperone me?"' I said, "I've gone through that, you're a big girl. It's fine, it's safe." And she said, "Oh no, but I can't. I'm a woman, I can't travel by myself."'*

Sharon realised the only way she would attend was if her father travelled with her, so she made the appropriate arrangements. Back in Australia, however, they had difficulty grasping the concept.

> *'The conference organisers couldn't quite understand; they wondered if she was royalty or very young, or disabled. Why would someone need to be chaperoned, because it's so foreign for us. And I said, "Look, it's just a cultural thing."'*

A sense of achievement

Gaining experience in a small institution may not have given her the status of a top-ranked institution like the Juilliard School in New York; it did, however, provide her with breadth of experience and scope to teach her way, which she would not have been offered at larger schools. Now she could tick off on her list a range of achievements, including writing 20 new courses, teaching new subjects she would otherwise not have taught, establishing the *Malaysian Music Journal* in two languages and starting up a Western orchestra from scratch.

She also took the opportunity to travel extensively throughout Malaysia, Asia and, at the end of her stay, Europe.

> *'I went there with a list of things I wanted to achieve and I'd actually achieved them all. The next step for me would be to become a full professor, but that would be five or six years. I thought I needed a new challenge.'*

So after two years of extraordinary experience, Sharon set her sights on coming home to Australia.

Back home

Heading back home, Sharon was surprised to find the adjustment took longer than she expected. A form of reverse culture shock hit her when she realised she was free to walk down the street on her own without being accosted by men. Then there was the spare time she had back in Australia. In Malaysia, she would have to put aside half a day for simple mundane chores, like visiting the post office or paying bills. Back in Melbourne, she put aside half a day and had it done within 15 minutes. She remembers standing on the street at a loss, not knowing what to do with the remaining time. Being on first-name terms with academics also seemed strange for a while.

In Melbourne, Sharon was surprised at how easy it was to re-establish her music practice, when several students contacted her once they heard she had returned. She also energetically applied for academic roles across Australia, and was accepted into the University of Tasmania for a maternity leave replacement. Serendipitously, at the end of her 12-month appointment she was offered a job back in Melbourne at the Australian Council for Educational Research, where she worked for about one year. She was then approached by Charles Darwin University for a lecturer position. This role was, in fact, one she had turned down to take up the maternity leave role in Tasmania, and now the time was right to accept.

Sharon's reflections

Sharon's advice to women considering moving overseas is to be prepared — you will have lonely times, and your whole life will likely change. Make the effort to seek out friends, develop interests outside of work and have a well-rounded experience. It can be very lonely in that small apartment after the workday is finished, and it can be difficult to handle the exclusion you'll feel by being an outsider. Seek out a local mentor to show you around, and to help you navigate the cultural nuances and move up the learning curve much faster. By adopting these practices Sharon was alone, but never lonely.

Were the experiences and the hardships worth it? Absolutely. If she hadn't gained that overseas experience in Malaysia, she's convinced she would not have been offered any of the roles back in Australia. She is also richer for the cultural experience, which at times tested her own values and beliefs.

Perhaps Mahatma Gandhi had the last word about cultural integration and acceptance when he said in 1921, 'I want the cultures of all lands to be blown about my house as freely as possible. But I refuse to be blown off my feet by any.'

Sharon is still enjoying her lecturing post at Charles Darwin University and, best of all, it's a tenured position. She feels that she's made it.

Lucy Roland

Success is the Best Revenge

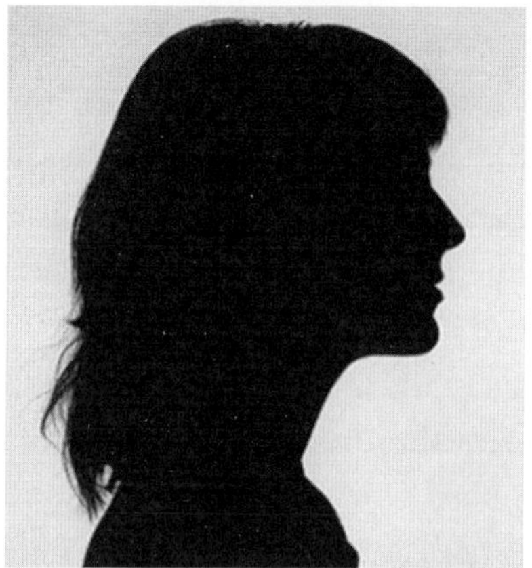

Lucy Roland has more than 20 years of experience as a business development and marketing specialist and communications coach. She has worked across the commercial, not-for-profit and government sectors, including professional and financial services, IT and community services organisations.

Note: The names and identifying details in this chapter have been changed to protect the privacy of individuals.

Off the radar

> *'You're done for, now that you're having a child. Really, you're off our radar now as talent.'*

These were the words that bowled Lucy over when she met with Rupert, her manager in a highly successful global business, Newbizz, to discuss plans around her pregnancy and return to work.[1] She was in line to become the next Head of Marketing — she was on the succession planning charts for this role, had a development plan in place to prepare her for the position and had been given promises that it would happen. When she became pregnant, Rupert flippantly said, 'Well, obviously you won't be Head of Marketing now.'

Rupert had been Lucy's manager in a previous firm and headhunted her into Newbizz three years after he joined the firm. He knew she was a top performer and a hard worker, smart, loyal and dedicated to her career. He supported Lucy in completing a Masters of Marketing at the University of Melbourne, a degree costing Newbizz $30,000. Then, just as she completed her degree, she threw a spanner in the works and got pregnant. 'Well, there's $30,000 down the drain,' mused Rupert.

When it started, Newbizz was a pioneering business with a strong, innovative culture and strategy of growth through aggressive global acquisitions that saw it become one of the fastest growing businesses in Australia. With all that creative thinking and a ground-breaking approach to business growth, how did this firm allow one of its most respected and highest performing women leaders to fly the coop?

The best plans are spontaneous

Lucy and her husband, Gavin, have a loving partnership — they are very close, enjoy each other's company and live a comfortable life. Welcoming two beautiful daughters into their lives added another dimension. However, they are not totally obsessed with their children and balance out family time, partner time and personal time as best they can. It sounds like a healthy mix.

Gavin and Lucy are both spontaneous in their approach to life and work. Both children were born after only brief conversations about the possibility of starting a family.

Lucy's approach to her career was similarly unplanned and evolutionary. A few years after having completed a Bachelor of Arts, her passion for sales and marketing was kindled by a chance role. Lucy then travelled overseas, where she worked for a year in a social justice organisation, focusing on the provision of services in the Council flats of London. She would return to the community sector later, drawing on her passions for sales, marketing and social justice, first experienced in these early years.

You can't be what you can't see

Rupert's response to Lucy's pregnancy was all the more surprising, as she had already taken a full 12-month period of maternity leave at Newbizz with her first child. However, the situation was somewhat different the first time. She was at a more junior level in the business then, and reported to a female manager, Jennifer, who also had children. On the other hand, Jennifer was not the perfect role model when it came to taking an extended period of maternity leave, returning to work six weeks after having her first child. So when Lucy elected to take a full 12 months maternity leave it was, relatively speaking, a long break from the business.

On her return to work, Lucy was given a three day a week role managing a small team, at which she performed exceptionally well and received great feedback from the business.

This was the period when her salary and Gavin's started to diverge, and with it her status in the firm, although she hadn't realised it at the time.

Jennifer was promoted from Director of Marketing in Australia to head up an operation in South Africa soon after Lucy returned to work. After much deliberation, Rupert decided to give Lucy about 80 percent of Jennifer's responsibilities, but without the title or the salary. This was put to her as a 'great opportunity'. She didn't argue — it probably was, she thought at the time.

However, Lucy noticed a change in Rupert's behaviour that worried her. In effect, Rupert began a campaign of passive resistance against her, which had the effect of sabotaging her career. A tell-tale sign was when Rupert repeatedly 'forgot' to advise the management team of Lucy's new responsibilities, despite promises to do so on several occasions. This lack of communication with the executive team completely disempowered her and undermined her authority with them. Lucy can only speculate about the reasons for this behaviour. Possibly, Rupert was hoping Jennifer would return soon. Perhaps this was a demonstration of his belief that mothers are unable or unworthy to deal with a demanding career. After all, Rupert's wife was a stay-at-home mum and gave up her career for their children. Maybe he thought Lucy would turn into a baby-making machine, having had two children in short succession! Whatever the reason, Lucy was exposed to the full force of Rupert's disapproval.

This disapproval seemed to extend to her team, too. The first time she became pregnant, her team were thrilled and excited for her, giving her a resounding farewell and showering her with gifts. In comparison, the second time she just quietly packed her boxes and slinked out of the office without any celebration or goodbye. She recalls it as one of her saddest days.

Unrealised potential

Newbizz had recently acquired a major business in Germany. Many Australian employees were going over to Germany to manage the transition and Lucy could have been one of them — she was available, eager and experienced, and would have relished the idea of working overseas for a few years. Unfortunately, those opportunities took place during the time she was pregnant and on maternity leave, and when she was reporting to Rupert. 'Oh well, you won't be going overseas now,' Rupert had said when he heard she was having another baby. Yet:

> *'If we had been posted to the US and I had been in a full-time role there, Gavin would have been more than happy to be the carer of the children at home. But we never got to have that conversation with Newbizz because they made an assumption that I would always want a part-time role.'*

Instead, she would be offered a Special Projects role on her return from maternity leave — 'a real kick in the guts', Lucy recalls.

How could an organisation that had invested in someone so talented write her off? The business was deadline-driven — a neat explanation and justification to retain the status quo around long working hours and face-time in the office. However, there was no conversation with her about what the business needed, where there could be meaningful opportunities for Lucy to contribute, or how she could work around the peaks and troughs in demand. The financial and economic impact within the business was huge, says Lucy, particularly when there could have been a very straightforward process for identifying a different way of working that could have grown her capabilities and created significant pay-off for the business. Rupert simply chose not to think outside the box, and so they lost a highly valuable resource.

Powerlessness in the face of a powerful elite

Knowing Lucy as a fearless, outspoken and confident woman, there is no doubt she would have stood up for her rights today. But back then she was younger, inexperienced and lacked the support from the business to challenge these decisions.

Lucy was also caught up in a boys' club that would have been hostile to any challenge to one of its own. The executive team were all mates, and the 'usual clichés' applied in the workplace. Apart from the Head of Human Resources and the Chief Financial Officer, who were women, men controlled the business. There was lots of drinking, smoking, 'bonding' through frequent overseas travel or on the golf course, and crass jokes and innuendo were considered just normal office banter. Rupert was part of this tight-knit team of senior executives, men whose power was explicit and who controlled and shaped the destiny of the business. It is unlikely any challenge to his behaviour would have been taken seriously.

Lucy was also not aware of her rights, and challenging a powerful senior executive on her own was too much to expect. The Human Resources department took no action to advise her of these rights or support her in asserting those rights. She didn't understand that what had just happened was illegal and, like many of us, was learning as she went along.

Finally, it can be very difficult to openly challenge subtle forms of passive resistance from a senior manager. It would have been easy to tell herself she was over-reacting and give Rupert the benefit of the doubt.

Rejection was the best thing that could have happened

When it came time to return to work, Lucy just couldn't face the idea of taking on the Special Projects role after the promises of promotion and the tantalising opportunities for overseas experience evaporated. She knew she had skills in demand and, after her experience working in social justice in the UK, realised she had always wanted to work in the not-for-profit sector. So, with Gavin's support, she resigned from Newbizz and established her own business development and marketing consulting business.

> *'The irony of the whole situation is that I like being a small business owner, but I never would have chosen it for myself unless I had been forced into it.'*

She's satisfied with her decision, except occasionally when that little green-eyed monster raises its ugly head and says, 'See that exciting overseas trip Gavin has just got? That could have been you!'

Women coming into their own

Women are leaving the corporate world in droves to establish their own businesses. According to one Dun & Bradstreet survey the number of women running their own business doubled between 2007 and 2012, when it hit the one million mark. Of these women, 78 percent came from middle to upper management jobs in corporates.[2] Research by the Australian Women's Chamber of Commerce & Industry (AWCCI) indicates that 34 percent of women who started their own business in Australia did so to pursue work-life balance and flexibility, while 12 percent did so to escape the corporate world.[3]

Not only are women starting up their own businesses, they are outperforming men. According to US research spanning 14 years to 2011, businesses owned by men grew by 25 percent, half the growth rate of businesses owned by women; revenue growth from women-owned businesses also outperformed men-owned businesses.[4] We know that Australia produces more female graduates than men (57 percent of higher education students are women).[5] What a waste of talent when entrepreneurial businesses deny women the opportunity or actively discourage them from re-entering the workplace.

Mind the gap

Anyone striving to move up the corporate ladder will recognise that there is a relatively small window, perhaps five or so years, which can make or break a career. If you're in the right organisation you can move ahead in leaps and bounds, but if you're in the wrong place at the wrong time it can prove fatal. The median age for first-time mothers in Australia is 30 years,[6] just when women are starting to be recognised in the workplace — often they are on fast-track promotion paths and being identified as high performers at this time, yet not senior enough to be able to call the shots around their working arrangements. Their careers may be interrupted for one year, or up to five years if they have more than one child, a relatively short time in terms of their whole working life, but critical in the trajectory of the talent pool. By putting their career on hold they often lose their place in the talent pool, while others without family responsibilities move on and up. Not only has their career stalled, others may question their competence in later years as they will have taken longer to get to senior roles, compounding the gap even further. Perhaps it's not surprising that women are having children later in their careers in order to safeguard this critical period.

Lucy reflects on Gavin's workday. As a senior executive in a highly successful insurance business, Gavin works long hours, travels frequently, but can do the school drop-off or pick-up between work responsibilities without feeling like he needs to slink off and hope no-one notices his absence. Seniority has its advantages.

Stereotypes are meant to be broken

Children are constantly being bombarded by gender stereotypes — just visit a toy store and you'll see gender segregation in the extreme. While it's impossible to completely prevent children from being exposed to the gender expectations society places on them, Lucy is determined to balance out messages whenever she can. That's why she believes it's important for the girls to see Lucy enjoying work and succeeding, as well as being a good mother and a happy, independent person in her own right. She wants to be a role model to the girls, so they develop their own independent lives, choosing and pursuing work they love rather than being dependent on the stereotypical 'male as breadwinner' model.

Having an office at home is something many people envy, but it is also a potential danger, where Lucy can easily fall into the stereotypical female role of doing the household chores while the dad comes home with the pay packet at the end of the day. It's therefore critical that Gavin and Lucy plan and divide responsibilities up according to their capacity to do them, to fight against perpetuating the conventional division of responsibilities or placing the burden of childcare disproportionately on Mum.[7]

Each weekend they plan the following week's responsibilities around school pick-ups, the children's activities and domestic chores. They also have a safety net if things go wrong — they don't have family close by, but do have a network of friends and neighbours in the local community who help each other out. She is also highly respectful of women who choose to stay home to care for their children, though it's not her preference.

Reflections

The best piece of advice Lucy can give a woman struggling with the work/family conundrum is to be clear about what you want your world to be like and then develop a practical plan to get there. Talk to as many people as you can about your ideas and explore opportunities with them. Ultimately, we have to live with the choices we've made, so make sure you have thoughtfully identified and evaluated them. Don't be a victim of circumstance; make choices, take ownership of them and accept the outcomes.

Lucy also fervently believes that workplaces need to take the focus away from women and mothers, towards creating genuine workplace flexibility for all employees so everyone can bring their whole being to work. We need a broader conversation about how we operate as a community, and how we enable people to maintain lives that are fulfilling at work and outside of work. This means addressing deep-seated cultural barriers and entrenched power bases around what the workplace should be like, breaking down cultural norms around the roles men and women take on at work, and how men and women should work together.

Breaking down gender stereotypes challenges businesses to be innovative in their work practices. Businesses who refuse to consider realistic flexible working arrangements for their employees are shooting themselves in the foot — research shows that women in flexible roles waste less time at work and are actually more productive than men and women in full-time working arrangements.[8]

Discouraging women to return to work costs the nation billions of dollars in unrealised productivity potential and higher government benefit payments. Melbourne's Grattan Institute has estimated that if women in Australia had the same participation as women in Canada our GDP would be about $25 billion higher by 2022.[9] I can't resist concluding this chapter with a quote from Sheryl Sandberg, Facebook COO, who found that when she cut back her office hours dramatically after having children she was not just working less, but was more productive.

> *'Having children forced me to treat every minute of my time as precious — did I really need that meeting? Was that trip essential? And not only did I get more productive but everyone around me did too as I cut out meetings that weren't essential for them also.'*[10]

It's time businesses and our country started reaping these productivity bonuses.

Contemporary Research

Dr Hannah Piterman

The Career Interruption that has No Name

Dr Hannah Piterman is the director of HPCG and is a consultant and advisor to senior management and boards in the areas of governance, leadership and diversity.

Hannah designs frameworks for good governance, conducts board evaluations, undertakes organisation reviews, advises on diversity and coaches executives across a wide range of industry sectors, including health, education, media, finance, construction and professional services.

Hannah's consulting assignments and research undertakings have led to published reports and articles in the media, business publications and international peer-reviewed journals. She is a regular presenter and facilitator on leadership at business forums in Australia and internationally.

Prior to becoming a consultant, Hannah held senior positions in industry, university and government sectors.

Hannah is an adjunct Associate Professor at Monash University. She is a Member of the Committee of Economic Development of Australia (CEDA) Victorian/Tasmanian Advisory Council, Member of the Project Advisory Committee for the InTouch support for CALD women experiencing family violence, Member of the Business Network Committee of the Jewish Museum of Australia (JMA), and Chair of the Advisory Board of Project Deborah. She is a past Member of the Advisory board of the Anti-Defamation Commission.

> *'They are words you don't hear in everyday talk at the office or at your weekly "Mommy and Me" class. That's because domestic violence prefers to keep hidden behind closed doors and drawn curtains. It feels most comfortable lurking in the shadows, in whispers, downcast eyes, and long-sleeve shirts.'*[1]

Women take breaks from work for reasons that include children, vacation, study and illness, often with the support of their employers, for leave such as family leave, study leave, sick leave and recreational leave. In most cases, women publicly acknowledge their reasons for taking leave. But when women have unscheduled work interruptions because of domestic violence they may not be willing to identify this to their employer or work colleagues, presenting other reasons for stepping out of the workplace. Most Australian businesses have no specific data on how the issue of violence against women may affect their operations. Traditionally, domestic violence has been treated as a personal matter that has no relevance to work. Managers have been reluctant to 'pry' into personal matters that are 'not their business', and workers are reluctant to disclose incidents of domestic violence for fear of losing their jobs.[2]

This paper intertwines the experiences of two women, Dianne and Kristen,[3] reflecting the unpalatable, complex dynamics in abusive intimate partner relationships, which see women's quality of life, sense of self and careers undermined. These women reflect on a work history that saw them take unscheduled career breaks, including sick leave, reneging on job opportunities and resigning from positions because of their experience of domestic violence. The women did not disclose the true reasons for taking leave or for reneging on job offers to their employers. They also did not disclose to family members, friends and even to themselves. A combination of fear, denial, shame and identification with the abuser created a situation in which domestic violence was a dark secret. Moreover, societal discomfort with crimes against women — a 'don't ask, don't tell' attitude — reinforced the status quo.

Dianne: 'My work promotion involved interstate travel. Ronald told me point blank that I was not to travel interstate. So I avoided going on interstate trips, even though it was essential for my work. On one occasion I was so terrified that Ronald would find out that I was booked to go to Sydney that I didn't turn up at the airport and missed my flight. I then called into work saying I was sick. I was continually fearful that I would be caught out doing something Ronald did not approve of. My work was suffering, as were my work relationships. Ronald said that work was making me a "stress bag". So I resigned. I was convinced that I needed a break. I felt my boss and work colleagues believed that I wasn't able to cope with the promotion.'

Kristen: 'John controlled all the money because he said I was hopeless with money. I allowed him because I knew that to challenge him would make things much worse at home. One day he discovered that I had spent money on a year's gym membership without asking his permission. When I came home he pushed my head against the wall and threatened that he would break me if I ever spent money without first checking with him. I tried reasoning with him. I said that I'm a "low maintenance woman" compared to other women. I could not go to work the next day or the day after or the day after that. I took a week's sick leave. I had tried to talk to my GP but he was not open to listening and wasn't all that direct. I needed to protect John. The hardest thing for me was pretending that everything was okay.'

Domestic violence — an epidemic

Violence against women is widely recognised as a global issue. It is an often invisible, but common form of violence, and an insidious violation of human rights. More than 39 percent of women in Australia aged over 18 have experienced violence at the hands of a man since the age of 15.[4] The experience of abuse is not confined to particular postcodes or statuses in society. Men in positions of authority, such as doctors, clergy, government ministers and judges, are not immune from being perpetrators and enablers.[5] Intimate partner violence is responsible for more ill health and premature death in Victorian women under the age of 45 than of any other well-known risk factors, including high blood pressure, obesity and smoking.[6] The violence can be physical, sexual, economic and psychological.

When the unspeakable bears no witness, reality becomes elusive to both abuser and victim. Out of sight violence continues unabated, propelled by righteousness, rancour and force, until in some cases it causes death. In Australia, a woman between the ages of 15 and 44 is murdered every week at the hands of her partner or an ex-partner.[7] Since early 2015, two women have been killed every week.[8]

Women with a history of domestic violence have a more disrupted work history and are consequently on lower personal incomes, have had to change jobs more often and are employed at higher levels in casual and part-time work. Between 25 and 50 percent of women who have been subjected to domestic violence report having lost a job, at least in part due to the violence.[9]

> *Dianne: 'I was losing concentration. This was a job that I had been able to do with my eyes closed, and now it was becoming too difficult. I began to dread work, dread friends and dread my parents. I decided to leave work because I was not coping. Everyone at work just assumed I had made the decision to be a full-time mum.'*

> *Kristen: 'We had few friends. My friends kept away. He was belligerent and lost jobs because of it. John couldn't get work in Melbourne. He eventually got a job in risk management with a local council in Darwin and we moved. I had been offered work at [one of the large professional services organisation] but when we got to Darwin John wouldn't let me take the job. He said childcare was too expensive without family support in Melbourne. So I had to decline the offer.'*

Misogyny, the building block of violence against women

It is the ubiquity of ordinary sexism that creates the circumstances for violence against women, and sees it as the leading cause of death and disability. Indeed, the most consistent predictor of the use of violence among men is their agreement with sexist, patriarchal, and/or sexually hostile attitudes.[10] This is reinforced by a culture of unequal distribution of power and resources between men and women, and an adherence to rigidly defined gender roles and identities, i.e. what it means to be masculine or feminine.[11]

> *Dianne: 'He criticised the way I did things around the house, even the way I cut the carrots, for God's sake. I found myself making sure that I cut up carrots before he came home. I didn't wanted to annoy him, but whatever I did or said ended up setting him off.'*

> *Kristen: 'When our first child was born I wasn't able to breastfeed. He saw this as my failing. The first time he became physically violent was when he saw me giving Jason a bottle. He threw a glass at the wall and it ricocheted, just missing us, before it hit the table and shattered, cutting my leg. I felt cowed and vulnerable. I lived in terror that he would hurt me and there would be no-one. I felt like I was walking on eggshells.'*

A culture of shame and blame

Most incidents of domestic violence go unreported. Women are even less likely to report violent incidents to police when the perpetrator is a current partner.[12] Rather than shining the light on men's behaviour, too often women are portrayed in the media as explicitly or implicitly eliciting their abuse and murder.[13]

Sadly, women internalise societal attitudes of blame, with a resultant damage to self-esteem and sense of identity. At its heart are feelings of shame. Hence when men abuse their partners for 'being crazy', 'a bad mother' and 'at fault', women believe they have failed as women.

> *Dianne: 'When I broke down he called me a "crazy wreck", "an unfit mother" and threatened to have me committed to "the lunatic asylum". I felt increasingly desolate and isolated. I was pervaded by a constant sense of foreboding that wouldn't leave me. I feared losing the children if I couldn't get myself together.'*

It is one of the significant reasons why women don't always report acts of violence to police, exacerbating isolation and stigma.[14] Shame and fear of being judged negatively is also a major reason why less than 30 percent of women disclose abuse to health professionals. Other reasons for lack of disclosure are fear of the abuser and a hope that things will change.[15]

Australia has a long way to go in shifting a culture of blame and shame, and the associated silence. While domestic violence is acknowledged as a crime, the lingering sense remains that women have provoked the attack by their failure to meet a societal ideal as mothers and wives. This is reinforced in a societal context where power relations between the sexes are unequal, normalising a patriarchal culture in which men's role as judge and enforcer in both the societal and private spheres is acceptable.

Shifting landscape

There is still much to do to identify incidents of abuse, prosecute offenders, and help victims of domestic violence. Attitudes, however, are shifting.[16] A greater community awareness of violence against women is creating a fertile ground for change. Much has changed since the times when the police and the courts viewed spousal abuse as an intractable interpersonal conflict unsuited for police attention, inappropriate for prosecution and substantive punishment.[17] Domestic violence is now an Australasian policing priority.[18]

Role of government

Governments at all levels are active in their focus on the outcomes of prevention and early intervention, victim safety and perpetrator accountability, providing a gateway for those experiencing family and domestic violence to access services and enabling courts to make domestic violence protection orders to protect victim safety. Support services include 1800RESPECT, Kids Helpline, Lifeline, MoneySmart and MensLine, among others.[19]

Role of workplaces

Domestic violence is a business issue. It is responsible for workplace problems such as absenteeism, lower productivity, higher turnover and excessive use of medical benefits. Two thirds of women who report violence by a current partner are in paid employment. The results of a national domestic violence and workplace survey conducted in 2011 found that 19 percent reported that family violence continued in the workplace, with 12 percent indicating it occurred in the form of abusive phone calls and emails, and 11 percent stating that it occurred by way of the violent person attending the workplace.[20]

As good corporate citizens, organisations need to be at the forefront of preventative actions that ensure the promotion of gender equality and development of respectful attitudes within their organisations, and to be role models in the wider community. Men's violence against women is sustained in part by institutional and collective factors and forces.[21] The way women and men are portrayed in the media and in advertising has an impact on the perception and treatment of women.

A number of Australian businesses have introduced initiatives to raise awareness and support women. These include the display of public education materials and helplines about domestic violence in accessible areas (e.g. kitchen, bathrooms, staff intranet), the offering of regular awareness training and education to all levels of the organisation about domestic violence, and guidance on how to handle disclosure of domestic violence. A number of large Australian organisations, including Telstra, National Australia Bank, Origin Energy, Commonwealth Serum Laboratories, Virgin Australia and BHP Billiton, have introduced polices that enable women to access domestic violence leave. An estimated 1.6 million people have accessed this policy.

Workplaces have been increasingly aware of the importance of development of organisational policies and procedures to ensure a safe, supportive and inclusive environment for women. A culture of equality enables the conditions that work against violence occurring by empowering bystanders (whether organisations or individuals) to stop perpetration of specific incidents of violence, reduce the risk of violence escalating, and prevent the physical, psychological and social harms that may result.[22] At an organisational or community level, a bystander approach can involve encouraging staff members to report incidents of violence or harassment, and having clear policies in place for responding to specific incidents. This includes engaging in programs such as the Take a Stand Partnership Program[23] that aims to change attitudes and behaviours that lead to violence against women, and the Australian Football League's (AFL's) Respect and Responsibility strategy that recognises the AFL's wider role in creating a safe and supportive environment for women.[24]

Role of individuals

As women we need to recognise the precursors of violent relations in our own partners, and those of our family and friends. We need to be vigilant to signs of control, pathological jealously, the way our partners talk about other women, a history of aggression and violence, and attempts to distance us from friends and family. We must be aware of our own negative self-talk (e.g. 'I must have done something to provoke him.') or the false belief that we have to put up with the violence in order to keep the family together, or that he will change.

> *Dianne: 'When we'd go out to dinner with friends he was the epitome of charm, but nasty behind their backs. He would say things to me like, "Keep away from Trish. She's not your friend."*
>
> *Ronald was livid with jealousy at my promotion. He accused me of having an affair with my boss; I was a ruthless whore who was sleeping her way to the top. He would ring me at work wanting to know what I was doing. On one occasion I saw him across the road from our office. He was spying on me. When I came home that evening he was in a paranoid rage.'*

Kristen: 'John didn't like me going out. He rang me five times a day for a blow-by-blow account of what I did, particularly what money I spent.

I felt partly to blame for John's behaviour. I was smarter and more successful, and I was making John feel inadequate. What kept me going was the belief that if I could manage everything — the house, the garden and work — while John got his act together and found a job, all would turn out well.'

As individuals we can no longer collude with the silence. We must shed shame and fear, and speak up for ourselves, our daughters, our friends and work colleagues. Women who are victims of domestic violence need to become informed, talk to a friend, family member or health professional about the abuse, and acquaint themselves with available resources and helplines. They need to contact police if they have been assaulted or threatened, and seek a restraining order prohibiting the abuser from contacting them or being near their homes or workplaces. Importantly, women need to develop a safety plan with the help of a friend or advocate. A woman is often in the most physical danger when she attempts to leave.

Those of us who bear witness must be encouraging, supportive and, most importantly, non-judgmental. If we believe someone is in an abusive relationship we can make ourselves available to listen. Sadly, we still have a way to go in managing a culture of blame, as evidenced by Rosie Batty, who recently commented that it is not uncommon for people who are supposed to be supportive to make harsh judgments.[25]

Dianne: 'Ronald would occasionally call me at work and abuse me. I was aware that it was a small office and Gillian [a work colleague] could overhear the conversation. I constantly apologised to Gillian at Ronald's ranting calls. She said, "Dianne, they get upset with all the pressure they have at work. You can't burden men with problems and never ever let yourself go."'

We need to be vigilant of signs of emotional withdrawal and physical injury in work colleagues, family members and friends. We can no longer remain as bystanders to men like Ronald and John, who we suspect of being violent. There is a mistaken belief that in instances of actual or potential violence we can intervene and possibly expose ourselves to personal harm, or we can mind our own business and do nothing. There are other options. As individuals we can offer support to someone who we know is experiencing abuse by listening to them, supporting them by contacting an appropriate service, or we can report an incident of violence to an appropriate authority if safe to do so.

A culture of zero tolerance for violence against women in all domains must exist — in the home, in the workplace and on the street. As Marilyn French said some years ago, 'As long as some men subjugate women, all men need not. The knowledge that some men can, and do, suffices to undermine all women.'[26]

Dr Jennifer Whelan

Work-life: Balance or Integration?

Dr Jennifer Whelan is the founding director of Psynapse Psychometrics and an Honorary Fellow at the Melbourne Business School. Innovative and outcomes-driven, Jennifer combines her depth of research expertise and organisational experience to provide evidence-based organisational change and leadership development programs.

Her work focuses on enabling organisations to realise the benefits of organisational diversity and inclusion. In her consulting and advisory work, Jennifer helps leaders and organisations develop the culture and capabilities that leverage diversity and inclusion and enable organisations to grow their collective intellectual capital.

Jennifer provides consulting expertise, thought leadership, tailored assessment programs, and executive development programs on diversity, inclusive leadership, and innovation to some of Australia's largest organisations. Jennifer is also an active thought leader and a regular contributor to industry forums, events, media, and public debate, including engagements with the Committee for Economic Development of Australia (CEDA), the Diversity Council of Australia (DCA), Women in Banking and Finance (WiBF), the Property Council of Australia, and the 100% Project.

Introduction

Work-life balance, or flexible work, is one of the most prominent areas of organisational focus in the human resource domain. This is arguably even more so the case in relation to diversity and inclusion initiatives. In fact, many large organisations have devoted substantial effort to promoting and enabling flexible work practices, with a specific view to increasing women's professional participation.

While flexibility is arguably a key component of the diversity agenda, the association of work-life balance initiatives with diversity and inclusion practices can in reality be counter-productive. Many organisations have struggled to encourage men to consider flexible work because it is assumed to be for women with family commitments. Indeed, as the following chapter will show, there are particular dynamics involved when it comes to men who want to work more flexibly, and particular reasons why tying flexibility to the diversity agenda may get in the way of mainstreaming work-life balance.

This chapter will review work-life balance initiatives in large organisations, particularly with respect to their role in diversity and inclusion, and the changing nature of work, for both men and women.

Work-life balance and women's workplace participation

The focus on flexibility within the gender diversity and inclusion agenda cannot be understated. Virtually every large or publicly listed Australian organisation has flexibility as a key strategy on its diversity and inclusion agenda. Some have embraced the task with more innovation and enthusiasm than others, but the idea that work-life balance is a critical element to improving women's career trajectories is pervasive.

For good reason, women have been a key driver of the focus on flexibility. They make up between 40 to 60 percent of employees and a majority of the educated talent pool in most developed countries.[1]

Men have not been as quick to 'lean in' on the domestic front as women have been on the professional one; men spend twice as much time as women in paid work outside the home, and half as much time as women on unpaid work inside the home.[2] But times are changing there, too. While anecdotally, many people comment that generation-Y women are less concerned about gender equality at work, both men and women from generation-Y expect to have greater gender equality in their personal relationships.

Of course, the more men who engage more equally in the domestic realm, the easier it is for women to participate more fully in the professional one, especially after they have had children. A more equal distribution of both domestic and professional labour between men and women will result in a range of benefits. On the one hand, women can reasonably expect to combine meaningful career progression and family commitments. On the other hand, men's greater participation at home provides a more meaningful and varied family experience. These two dynamics combine to dramatically alter the balance of traditional gender roles, norms and expectations for the next generation. This is by far the most effective way to minimise the impact of the unconscious (and conscious) biases and stereotypes that shoehorn both sexes into rigid moulds.

We'll return to men's take-up of flexible work a little later on. In the meantime, flexible work is considered key to diversity and inclusion in organisations largely because of the assumption that providing women with better return-to-work options after they have children will increase women's workforce participation. While some more progressive organisations aspire to mainstream flexible work for all employees, the majority of organisations typically position flexibility as a strategy for attracting and retaining female talent.

This assumption that flexibility increases women's participation is largely a sound one. Even when we consider the area of heaviest focus in the diversity arena — women in leadership — research by Catalyst in 2013 found that 83 percent of high-potential women aspired to C-suite roles in organsations offering flexible work options, compared to just 54 percent in organisations that didn't offer flexibility.[3] This suggests that flexibility not only enables women to combine career and family, but also increases their likelihood of advancement to senior roles.

However, the tying of flexibility to women's advancement has created an accompanying set of assumptions that are less useful for diversity and inclusion in general, and for women in particular. Women still make up the vast majority of part-time workers and, despite outnumbering men up to professional levels, there is an exodus of women from organisations at mid-management level.[4] This exodus is largely (though not entirely) a result of the coincidence of women's mid-career attainment with the stage in life that they are most likely to start a family.

Many women brace themselves for the stigma of the so-called 'mummy track' when they reach this point in their careers. The assumption that flexibility retains women is in part true, but it also reinforces the notion that most talented women will return in a flexible capacity, and as a result will be a bad development investment when it comes to advancement of high-potential consideration. While there have been some notable high-profile exceptions, such as part-time CEO of Morgan McKinley, Louise Langridge, this inadvertent reinforcement of the 'women-carer, men-breadwinner' stereotype has pigeonholed women with families as women who probably won't rise to the senior ranks. When it comes to women in leadership, these perceptions are a major barrier in the form of biases and assumptions about women's potential.[5]

The ideal worker myth

One of the most stubborn challenges to the mainstreaming of work-life balance is the myth of the 'ideal worker'. A largely unspoken assumption generally surrounds discussions about work-life balance: the ideal worker doesn't have a life outside of work that requires balancing to begin with. Therefore, balance is only something you need if you're non-mainstream. This is known as the ideal worker stereotype; anyone of ambition will tell you that the more you trade your professional life in favour of family priorities, the smaller your chances of advancement. That dynamic holds for both women and men, though it affects women more because of the expectation that they will become the primary carers of children.

Williams, Blair-Loy and Berdahl examined this ideal worker notion in 2013, widely held by managers, that work requires and deserves undivided and intense allegiance.[6] As a result of this assumption, any competing commitments, be they children, elderly parents or hobbies, are seen as problematic. This norm operates both at the level of managers' expectations of their employees, and also at the level of the 'ideal' employee's expectations of themselves. Many employees feel pressure to prioritise work at the expense of other important factors, and many have also internalised the myth of the ideal worker as part of their own work ethic.

While both men and women who do *not* have family responsibilities are at an advantage when it comes to fulfilling the ideal worker myth, there is an implicit message pervasive in organisations when it comes to flexible work practices. Part of the ideal worker archetype is the assumption that men are typically less likely to be burdened with domestic responsibilities than women, even after they start a family, and are therefore more likely to be 'ideal' compared to women.

Linda Wayman, Southern Cross Austereo Executive, is so troubled by flexible work that she keeps a jar of condoms in the office to deter female staff from starting families. While this is arguably a tongue-in-cheek gesture, she believes that a future in which work-life balance is the norm is too idealistic, that it is too difficult to manage, and she staunchly opposes any legislative attempts to make part-time work automatically accessible to women returning from maternity leave.[7]

In a sense, it is easy to sympathise with Ms Wayman's observations. Anecdotally, many women baulk at the prospect of advising their manager of a pregnancy. Similarly, it is not uncommon to hear senior managers tell of their exasperation on hearing the news that their new 'target-hired' female promotion is soon to be heading off on maternity leave and expects to return to her position part-time. The perception that women in the golden phase of their careers are more likely than men to take time off work to have children at a similar career stage is deeply ingrained, and not without reason. This highlights the supposition that flexibility is still primarily a challenge to the perceptions and capabilities of managers, rather than an operational problem.[8] That said, the nature of work is well and truly changing. Smart organisations and leaders have read the signs, and are adapting accordingly.

The changing nature of work, and life

The nature of work has changed immeasurably in the space of a single generation. Communication and technology, combined with an ever-increasing focus on leanness and efficiency as a competitive strategy, have transformed the way we work. Large organisations today have flatter hierarchies, are more cross-functionally collaborative, more geographically dispersed, more dynamic and adaptive, and typically engage in continuous cycles of change and restructure in an attempt to keep up with the pace of change in their operating environments.[9] Perhaps as a result, they are also less likely to provide life-long careers or long-term job security for their employees. The days of a 'job for life' have long gone.

Organisations have arguably reaped the lion's share of the benefits that technology has brought. For employees, however, it has been something of a double-edged sword. The ability to work from anywhere has also brought the expectation of constant availability. As a result, what organisations see as flexibility, many employees see as intrusion or inundation.

This rather one-sided outcome of technology may in part stem from the fact that, despite the dramatic technological changes, most large organisations still operate under models of employment practice that might now be more appropriate for a bygone era.[10] This old model of the employment contract was predicated on the idea that an employee is given financial compensation in return for offering a proportion of their time to performing a specified task. While these days a manager may reasonably expect a degree of out-of-hours email availability, they also still expect employees to be physically present at fixed times, on fixed routines, doing fixed tasks that often bear no tangible relation to operational requirements. Long hours with few objective measures of productivity are still the norm, despite ample evidence that people are more productive and engaged when they have more autonomy over how, when and where they work.

In fact, we might well ask that, given the revolution technology has enabled, why have workplaces and work cultures been so slow to adapt? While many organisations offer part-time work, compressed hours, flexible hours or job sharing, these 'cosmetic' adjustments are often seen as rewards or special benefits that managers routinely struggle to accommodate, and often see as a cost and inconvenience. Small tweaks offered selectively on a reactive 'needs' basis, primarily to mothers, are unlikely to overhaul our existing model of work and life.

Despite this, the rise of freelancing, self-employment, telework and portfolio careers points to a major shift in the way we work, and smart organisations are catching the tide. New ways of working are increasingly positioned in terms of productivity and competitiveness, and businesses that have been particularly successful in mainstreaming non-traditional ways of working have been motivated predominantly by operational imperatives: logistical and overhead costs, better access to consumers, geographical location streamlining and reducing staff costs. What they have also observed along the way, of course, are the side-benefits of mainstreaming flexibility: higher productivity, engagement, health and wellbeing, reduced absenteeism, sick leave and turnover.

Activity-based work at Medibank

For health insurance provider Medibank, the key drivers for mainstreaming flexible work were to embody the company's For Better Health purpose, along with more logistical goals, such as reducing its real estate footprint. The company has successfully introduced Activity-Based Work (ABW) across all areas in the organisation, and it has done this independently of any of its diversity and inclusion objectives.

The central goal was to promote the company's mission internally by acknowledging that better health and wellbeing starts with the everyday, and that for most people, the bulk of their days are spent at work. The necessary re-engineering of roles, processes, routines and physical workspaces was aimed at increasing employees' freedom of movement and choice, enabling greater flexibility and mobility, and improving creativity, collaboration, engagement and productivity.

Subsequent to introducing ABW, a large majority of staff have reported a stronger connection to the company's purpose, greater levels of collaboration, and better health, wellbeing and productivity. The company reported no differences between men and women employees in the transition to ABW, rather the differences were at the individual level, with people exercising greater freedom and mobility as a function of their role, lifestyle, age and stage in career and location. In combination with the presence of extensive flexible and part-time working models for men and women, the company also experienced an improvement in external talent attraction.

The transition has not been without its challenges. Technology and technical support functions were required to step up activity, and historically desk-bound processing roles required additional resources. At the personal level, old habits die hard, and predictable dynamics emerged around flexible workspaces and hot-desking at Medibank's new corporate locations. Reluctance to give up personal workspaces was one of these dynamics, with staff leaving belongings on desks to reserve them for later use.

Overwhelmingly, however, the benefits appear to have outweighed the negatives. As one leader working in product design observed, ABW 'has enabled people to talk to people who they wouldn't normally work with, and gain knowledge about a number of different areas of the business'. As a result, creativity and innovation have bloomed, different parts of the business have been brought together like never before, and the increased level of connection between people has fed into the company's culture.

As one of the first large Australian organisations to adopt activity-based work, the experience at Medibank is an enlightening one. When positioned as a core business imperative, and integrated into the culture, organisations can dramatically re-imagine the way they work, and enable both men and women to integrate work and life so they are complementary rather than mutually exclusive.

With thanks to Medibank for their participation in interviews

'Equilibrium men': When the ideal worker meets gender stereotypes

Men's use of flexible work options challenges the traditional masculine stereotype. Of course, many men do not fit the ideal worker mould, nor do they wish to, and many men who do dearly wish they could break free of it. Nonetheless, only 20 men for every 500 women per month have taken parental leave since the Labor government introduced their Paid Parental Leave scheme, which provided two weeks of government-funded pay to fathers or same-sex partners.[11]

There is little doubt that prevailing social norms and gender roles play a large role in men's reluctance to work flexibly. But there is an additional dynamic at play too, and organisations have been unwittingly complicit in it. As we observed at the beginning of this chapter, flexible work has been a central pillar of gender diversity initiatives in organisations. This has siloed flexible work as the preserve of women with family responsibilities. In so doing, there has been an additional consequence for men.

While all employees, male or female, are considered to be less ambitious and committed if they take up flexible work, this is disproportionately the case for men. In one of the few examples of 'backlash' in the organisational setting working against men rather than women, men who take up flexible work are stigmatised more than women because they are violating the masculine stereotype.

One of the reasons organisations struggle to mainstream flexibility is because men remain reluctant to embrace it. In a 2012 study conducted by the 100% Project, men who associated flexibility and work-life balance with women were less likely to request it, even in the presence of supportive policies and managers.[12] Most interestingly, this effect was found at the unconscious level, where most of our stereotypes operate. In other words, unconscious bias about the 'femininity' of work-life balance was the major obstacle to men's uptake. Ironically, organisations have accidentally reinforced this perception by connecting flexible work with gender diversity practices.

It is hard to tell whether men's reluctance to take up flexible work would be solved if it were normalised rather than gendered — would they work flexible hours in droves given a truly value-judgment-free choice? Precisely those questions are explored in a novel initiative by the Workplace Gender Equality Agency (WGEA) called *The Equilibrium Man Challenge*. The project is a documentary film that follows the experiences of a number of senior men in three different large organisations as they transition to flexible work options. Refreshingly, the men come from a range of backgrounds and industries, and not all are transitioning to flexible work for childcare reasons. Providing compelling narratives of men's experiences can only serve to help dispel the assumption that 'real men' don't work flexibly.

Flexible work or a flexible career?

The archetype of the perfect employee only applies to a very small number of extremely ambitious people, those who are intrinsically driven to give their professional lives their undivided energy and attention. The problem, of course, is that managerial fantasies dictate that every employee should be one of these 'high potentials'. As a result, any work-life balance needs are viewed as a disqualifying factor when it comes to advancement. Work-life balance is code for 'I don't live to work', and these people don't tend to get ahead in a highly competitive professional environment.

There's no denying that, notwithstanding some high-profile exceptions, the majority of people, male or female, who choose to work part-time will reduce their chances of career advancement. It is axiomatic in most organisations that rising to the top means working longer and harder, and competing more aggressively for opportunities. However, a Catalyst report in 2013 found that over half of high potentials at even senior levels in surveyed organisations rank flexibility very important or extremely important to them. More promisingly, the report found that high potentials with access to flexible options had higher career aspirations than those without access.[13] It may well be that flexibility, as a mainstream phenomenon at even senior levels, will result from this demand-driven dynamic. When you consider, however, the rate of restructure in many large organisations, and the relatively short tenure for senior executives, I wonder if the idea of one single 'career path' won't die out sooner than we think.

Samone McCurdy

'You Did What?': Taking the Daddy Track

Samone McCurdy teaches at Monash University in the Department of Social Work. Presently concluding her doctorate research, Samone is part of the Gender, Leadership and Social Sustainability (GLASS) Research Unit and sits on the steering committee for the Social Inclusion and Social Sustainability Research Unit (SISPRU).

In 2010, Samone completed Honours research examining the experiences of sexual harassment and workplace bullying in Human Service Organisations.

Her PhD builds on her interest in gender justice, policy and the workplace, examining the barriers to caregiving for working dads and its relationships with women's wider gender equality. Her large sample survey is one of the first in Australia to explore parental leave and primary care of preschool children through the eyes of contemporary breadwinning fathers.

Samone has over 15 years' experience in Employee Engagement, Industrial Relations and Workplace Diversity, providing strategic HR and Gender Diversity advice within large-scale private enterprise and public sector organisations.

Samone is the recipient of the Monash University Jubilee Honours Scholarship (2010), an APA Postgraduate Research Scholarship and Faculty of Medicine Post Graduate Award for Academic Achievement (2011).

Few people would disagree that many women face barriers, if not outright discrimination, when they transition to the role of working parent. There is some emerging research, however, that suggests discrimination and unconscious bias in the workplace may not be entirely grounded in gender and it is the 'caring element', or more precisely the reduction in work intensity this entails, that drives the differential treatment and outcomes for men and women. This infers that the change point for improved gender equality may need to shift from a focus on becoming an 'employer of choice for women' to a more sophisticated understanding of gender and the re-construction of the ideal worker paradigm. Exploring this possibility is the next major challenge for the gender equality project, and one in which fathers and their work and care experiences are foundational. Unfortunately, the state of knowledge on the subject is minimal.

Fathers, work and care

Men as fathers have been a neglected area of research in the work and care debate. It has been more or less assumed that fathers are reasonably happy with the longstanding gendered division of paid and unpaid work. Working fathers, however, have rarely been asked directly about their experiences or expectations balancing caregiving alongside careers.

Fatherhood is changing. Both culturally and politically it is becoming more acceptable, if not expected, that fathers will participate in the care of their children.[1] To what 'degree' remains contested, however. In Australia we know very little about men's views and experiences beyond taking paternity leave (short-term leave taken by fathers at or around the birth of their children) or using flexible work practices to 'supplement' primary care from the mother.[2] Yet it is primary caregiving that involves stepping away from work for a period of time or reducing work intensity in order to provide care that is important to understand, for a number of reasons.

Firstly, it is a fundamental source of discrimination in the workplace for women. The Australian Human Rights Commission recently reported that 50 percent of working women will experience discrimination during pregnancy, Paid Parental Leave (PPL) or upon their return to work.[3] Secondly, it is the step away from work to care and the consequences of this in a workplace context that contributes most significantly to the 'motherhood penalty'. Finally, we know very little about this from fathers' perspectives, and the way in which the important decisions about who cares and who stays home are made within heterosexual couples. What we do know is that PPL has been available to all parents for some time, yet it is the road less travelled for working fathers. They rarely take up leave opportunities to step away from work as a primary caregiver, even in the presence of paid leave to do so.

For the last five years I have extensively studied these anomalies. I have always found it fascinating how (relatively) equal domestic arrangements in contemporary heterosexual couples prior to children quickly reduce to the 1950s model of the family, where the wife is the main carer and domestic chief and the father is the main earner, at least until the youngest child goes to school. This appears to occur in the majority of Australian couples, even if that is not what was intended. It is also the assumption upon which so many, if not all, work and family policy and programs appear to be founded.

The Fathers Work and Care (FWC) study examined the barriers and enablers to primary caregiving for working fathers of preschool age children. It assessed the main influences on the work and family arrangements made among contemporary heterosexual couples where the father is the primary earner of the family — the most common family composition in Australia with preschool children. Drawing on 951 survey responses from fathers and 14 interviews with couples, a number of findings emerged that are of direct relevance to the experiences of transitioning to working parenthood that are shared in this book.

Primary caregiving

Particularly since the introduction of government PPL in Australia, there has been a flurry of review on best practice models and a more intense focus on fathers. Yet very little attention has been given to establishing their level of interest in primary care in the first place.

A snapshot of the attitudes and beliefs measured by the FWC study are shown in Figure 1. These figures suggest fathers are indeed interested in primary caregiving. It also appears these aspirations for primary caregiving are unlikely to be realised. Less than 21 percent of fathers reported having had primary caregiving responsibility for any child in their working life. While almost all fathers in the sample took two to four weeks of leave after the birth of their youngest child, few reported taking such leave to be the primary carer. These results paint a picture of a work and family dynamic that may see fathers as locked into their role as the primary earner as mothers are locked out of the workplace. As one survey participant noted:

> *'Being a primary breadwinner as a father and having to spend long hours away from your children during their developmental years is exceptionally difficult, and personally I think it is much underrated in our society. I miss my kids lots when I'm at work, and generally only get any quality time with them on the weekends — otherwise I'm generally gone in the mornings just as they're waking up, and when I get home they're tired and at the end of their day … it's a very difficult role to balance and I wish I could give them more.'*
>
> *Survey respondent, 2013*

Figure 1

85% of fathers agreed they would step away from work to look after their baby for 3 months or more if there were no financial barriers.

87% of fathers agreed that each partner should have their own entitlement to Paid Parental Leave (PPL) for primary care.

> Almost 90% of fathers reported they felt pressure to earn the money for the family yet only 33% felt it was natural that they be the primary breadwinner when children come along.
>
> Only 16% of the sample felt that fathers were as accepted as carers in the workplace as mothers.

When asked what drove their primary caregiving decisions for their youngest preschool child, the majority reported 'financial viability' and their 'partner's preferences' to be the most decisive factors in making the primary care arrangements.

> *'I was fully prepared to be primary caregiver and happy to do so if needed, but ultimately we chose to let my wife do that prior to returning to her work part-time. If things had gone the other way and I was primary caregiver, we would have been financially worse off due to less PPL for males, and I think that's an unnecessary discrimination.'*
>
> *Survey respondent, 2013*

It was access to father-specific, highly compensated PPL that was reported as the most essential policy feature for fathers before they could consider taking up PPL for primary care. The higher the rate of pay on the policy the more likely fathers were to report they would take it.

Fathers expressed frustration with the gendered access to paid leave for primary care, without which contribution to care in a more substantial way beyond 'helping' the mother for a few weeks after birth was virtually impossible.

> *'Two weeks of parenting leave for fathers? This beggar's belief. Prevailing attitudes in Australian society are very out-of-date. Fathers are expected to provide for their family financially, but subcultures frown upon fathers who don't also provide domestic support.'*
>
> *Survey respondent, 2013*

> *'The most important role for a man in life, for our future generations, is fatherhood. Leave for this needs to be flexible, paid and for a much greater period than currently allowed.'*
>
> *Survey respondent, 2013*

These responses express fathers' willingness to take a step away from work to be a primary caregiver to their children. In fact, over 63 percent of fathers said they would sooner step away from work to care for a child less than 12 months of age than place the child in formal childcare. This is a critical finding because it not only supports previous findings that parents prefer informal or parental care for young children, but debunks the myth that fathers are not open to caregiving and would prefer someone else to do the caring.

Adequate policy measures that take into consideration fathers' primary earner role in a family would no doubt provide an opportunity to contribute to care in line with their (and their partners') work and care aspirations, and would positively contribute to a re-construction of caregiving as purely women's business. There is also an increasingly convincing body of evidence that highlights the social and cognitive benefits of caregiving by fathers that together make a strong case for some level of primary caregiving from the father.[4] Not the least of these is the direct support of mothers' return to work sooner rather than later.

A uniform industrial or statutory leave regime that incorporates primary caregiving by the father is yet to emerge in Australia.[5] This may well explain why Australia has relatively poor maternal workforce participation rates compared to other OECD countries, and the Nordic nations in particular.[6] A highly compensated, father-designated leave is a hallmark feature of policy in these countries, and has been attributed to the higher proportions of mothers in paid employment and the less gendered caretaking regimes in the Nordic belt.[7] Parental leave policy change can create dramatic effects on caregiving. When Iceland introduced its 3/3/3 policy — three months of ring-fenced leave for the father, three months for the mother and three for either parent — paternal participation in PPL rose from three percent to 31 percent of eligible fathers.[8]

We have a very weak PPL regime in Australia at both the government and private employer level, and certainly nothing like many international schemes that are designed to encourage, if not compel, a more equal distribution of caregiving among couples. Policy, however, is not likely to be the 'silver bullet' to engineer shared care between couples. This is evident when looking at the more universally available employment offerings, such as family-friendly/flexible work provisions. Even with a more uniform access for both fathers and mothers, utilisation is as gendered as PPL.

The FWC study respondents, for example, mirrored the patterns found elsewhere.[9] Fathers were more likely to use the non-structural flexible practices, such as changing start and finish times or using flex time, to 'supplement' care of their children. The use of the more structural flexibilities that move away from the full-time model of work, and would make shared caregiving possible, were far less common. In fact, more fathers reported not using any flexible practices at all over using part-time work, job share or compressed work weeks.

Why?

The interview data from the FWC study provides some poignant insight as to why these gendered patterns of caregiving may persist even when reasonable policy options are available.

While the survey noted the first hurdle is a financial one because fathers are more often than not the breadwinner in the family, comments from the survey hinted that policy at replacement rates of pay may not be decisive. Workplace factors in the form of an enabling environment in the immediate work climate (as opposed to culture), and most predominantly the leadership of the direct manager, appear to play a critical role in the final decision-making for both mothers and fathers.

'I'd like to be more confident that taking parental leave wouldn't adversely affect my job. Policy is one thing; your immediate manager's views could be different.'

'Working flexibly has a very negative impact on career/promotional prospects. Difficulties in working from home are also contentious.'

'There is no point having policies for Carer's Leave and Paternity Leave, etc. if in practice it is frowned upon for someone to take such leave.'

Survey respondents, 2013

The comments allude to an important undercurrent bubbling beneath the survey results, and an attempt to understand the push and pull factors of distributing earning and caring roles among couples. The workplace, and managers in particular, seem to have a considerable influence on the transition to working parenthood and who takes on the primary earning/primary caring roles. This is experienced by parents in the workplace as a series of implicit and explicit sanctions on caregiving that appear based on the ideal worker as full-time, always available and physically present.

The research show workplace influences on caregiving arrangements deeply affect the private decisions heterosexual couples make in two ways. Firstly, as an influence on the level of caretaking the father *can* provide. This is his 'care capability' and is dictated by the paid policies (and their structure) available at the workplace (or elsewhere) and the willingness of his manager to uphold, comply or promote them. Secondly, the workplace exerts influence through the mother, in particular the level of engagement with the workplace prior to maternity leave, and the tone and tenor of negotiations when they return. If a return to work is sought, her 'offer' (hours, the type of work she will do, etc.) then drives the amount of caregiving needed for the child. Any opportunity for a 'policy holding father' to provide primary care is enacted only when and if the mother decides to return to work and a 'care deficit' is created. We saw this in the case of Anna Burke and Tracey Spicer, for example, whose partners stepped in as primary carers on PPL when Anna and Tracey had to return to work.

What, then, determines a woman's decision to return to work? As it turns out, it is a highly individual and complex assessment. Many factors are included in the return to work conundrum, including their own personal schemas of a 'good' mother, and the amount and type of caregiving she should provide. This appears to compete with other factors that mothers weigh carefully. Returning to work must result in an acceptable outcome, taking into consideration the perceived quality of the substitute care available (including care from the father, which was generally considered the ideal), the enjoyment of the actual role, their career aspirations, financial need and gain, and the perceived implications of long leave on their relevancy, remuneration and work status. The decision to return to work, and by extension the amount of caregiving provided by the father, is highly dependent on the mother and her engagement with her employer.

> *'I'm looking at what the job is and if it's really really the job that I want to go back to or not, some jobs yes it's good, working in marketing yes it's fine, but sometimes not really, I don't like the job, so no I'd prefer to stay home the whole time ... if I have the opportunity to stay home, I will stay home.'*
>
> *Melissa, primary caregiver*

It is easy to see how the influence of the workplace, and managers in particular, can creep into this assessment. Managers were considered either 'good' or otherwise, and the manager's approach to work and family was associated with final arrangements couples made. It was also noted that different managers in the same organisation could yield two very different results, expressing the limits of policy, values and culture, and the powerful role subjective and unconscious bias may have on the actual distribution of work and care among the couple.

> *'I'm still with the same employer — but I've started a new position*

now where I've got different responsibilities and a different manager, so it's not quite as flexible as it was.'

Anthony, joint caregiver

'I have had "good" managers who understand, but there are a few people who still don't have good managers. They make faces when women have to rush home, or there's a phone call from childcare that your kid is sick, come and pick her up. The managers are really bad at that, but my manager has been really very good all the time; I didn't have issues.'

Kylee, joint caregiver

Interestingly, almost all couples agreed that the workplace was on balance more actively accommodating of women compared to men, in terms of leave or work adjustment to accommodate caregiving. This also came through in the survey comments and interviews.

'Workplace clearly discriminates fathers' opportunity for career advancement when it comes to caring of children. Whereas a female worker will still have opportunity to advance after coming back from maternity leave. I was told by my manager that I should re-think my career options because I have family responsibility.'

Survey respondent, 2014

'People are willing to juggle and adjust around women … and I guess, you know, it seems less so for a man.'

Mandy, primary caregiver

A related issue was the finding that family-friendly arrangements were considered a privilege or a 'favour' meted out by the manager and largely based on some subjective criteria. Sometimes this was provided as a result of 'special' characteristics of the employee, including trustworthiness, tenure and position, number of children, and relationship with the boss.

'... when you stay in the job for a while, you build up a few credits and then you can kind of ask for a few favours, you know ... if you're new in your job you don't ask for half a day off to go do something because you're worried that they'll think you're a slacker, whereas if you've been there for a couple of years they know you're good at your job. I guess there's a comfort level and you're kind of confident to be able to ask for those things that rely on your boss going, "Yes, that's okay."'

Sharon, primary caregiver

In other instances, the outcome of requests were attributed to the manager's characteristics.

'The newer, younger managers appear, are much more open to flexible arrangements ... Whereas the older managers don't understand why you shouldn't be at your desk nine to five, and they're the ones that look at you sideways.'

Noah, joint caregiver

'But he's an older gentleman though ... he's probably a bit more biased in his view of things but that sort of [negative] comment is what we would get from a lot of people I would find.'

Harry, joint caregiver

Asking for work adjustment or leave for care was a measured and premeditated decision where the likely 'consequences' were taken into consideration. In the survey and the interviews, operating outside the ideal worker framework and bringing care responsibilities into the equation at work clearly held significance in terms of the employees' value, their competence and potential promotion opportunities in the future. This is of course contra to the policy mandate and intent. Again, the negative judgments passed on employees when requesting work adjustments for caregiving was considered harder on fathers compared to mothers.

'With male, senior managers? Yeah, probably see [it] as a bit of a —

this guy's not serious about his career. He's a bit of a cop out, a bit weak. Yeah, give him a flexible work arrangement, but he's not going to be our next boss or whatever.'

Henry, joint caregiver

'... and it is unspoken and what I feel is that when it comes to all these policies of equal employment opportunity and things like that, I think it all talks about women. There is a discrimination against women if a woman as a mother, as a pregnant lady, is not being provided an opportunity to have time off or work part-time or work from home then honestly people will start jumping and talking about discrimination. But when it comes to men, I think it's social culture that the man is always considered the main breadwinner so he has to work no matter what.'

Lyndon, primary caregiver

This snapshot of the experiences of fathers shows just how deeply the ideal worker norm has penetrated the adult psyche and its far-reaching consequences in terms of the distribution of work and care, and likely wider gender equality. Traditionally, it has been men who have been able to more readily fit this ideal worker mould because they had wives at home taking care of the children, and work and home life remained very separate. While working mothers have been operating in the workplace for some time, they have always struggled to keep up with the expanding demands from the workplace. At the policy level their presence has been accepted and accommodated. At the behavioural level it appears to me more akin to being tolerated and they must keep up! Thus, in the absence of an acceptable alternative source of care suitable to the child's needs at various ages, they have ultimately taken (or been forced to take) a back seat in the workplace — usually relegated to lesser jobs, on lower pay, and with less visibility and influence than their male cohorts.

Importantly, the role of managers in this is becoming clearer, presenting as both an opportunity and a threat to wider gender equality. As the women in this book have shown, a successful career is not necessarily in lieu of successful motherhood. However, a successful career does rely on an alternate source of care for children, and more often than not undertaking a full-time, high-intensity work load. This was the essential barrier the working mothers in this group faced as they transitioned to working parenthood. This was also the experience of the FWC study sample when undertaking or imagining taking up a greater role in the care of their children, indicating that the motherhood penalty may in fact be a parental penalty. A daddy track, though less worn perhaps, appears just as real and detrimental in the contemporary workplace.

The future

With all this talk about motherhood penalties, daddy tracks and ideal workers, what's a girl to do? The first and most critical step is to understand that there is very little work for women left to do on this front. The 'heavy lifting' must now be done by organisations, to take a bold step and move beyond aspirations to be an 'employer of choice for women' and for the government to support it.

There is a vast difference between a gender-sensitive organisation and a gender-equal one. The latter does not occur by accident. After many years researching gender in the workplace, I have found there are some clear markers that indicate a gender-equal enterprise, and that serve as sensible goals for organisations to aspire to. Within a gender-equal organisation you would find a strong assumption that every worker of childbearing age will be a primary carer for a period of time. It would hold managers accountable for ensuring their employees understood and had access to the policies that would help them make the transition to parenthood, and then further to working parenthood. It would deliver these policies in ways that were consistent, measured and beyond the murky realms of subjective judgement and unconscious bias. Finally, it would ensure that taking such leave or making adjustments to work patterns to accommodate care would be normative practice and without (as far as practical) negative consequences or penalty. Though such an organisation does not yet exist, it is possible.

We once lived in a world where men were forbidden from attending the birth of their children. Now things have changed, yet no law or policy was passed to engineer this shift. There was instead a groundswell of demand from partners, married with institutionalised accommodation from hospitals, that together created a new norm. Men stepped up and stepped into this transformation, and there is every reason to believe they will do the same again. The question is whether organisations will also do the same.

Conclusions

Work-life Balance — The Impossible Dream?

'I do think women can have it all, but not all at the same time.'
— Quentin Bryce, former Governor General of Australia

Taking a career break is risky, as the women profiled in this book will testify. Tracy Spicer says that women need to 'fight like hell'. They need to make plans to return to their pre-birth levels of responsibility and into a role that will accommodate their new caregiving responsibilities. Lucy Roland was sidelined after having baby number two in spite of the company's significant grooming and investment in her MBA education. Maggie Evans-Galea was told upfront in her first post-doctorate position that having a baby was a 'career killer' in science, while by Lisa Croxford's own admission, her law firm was 'going out on a limb' to take her back under more family-friendly work conditions. These experiences make returning to work after having a child appear more like combat than transition.[1]

Many of the *Career Interrupted* women found themselves in a daily struggle with the goal of 'having it all': achieving a truly inspiring and rewarding career, having a healthy and spiritually rewarding life, while also being the best partners, mothers, sisters, daughters and employees they can be. Sometimes they felt so exhausted they wondered if it was all worth it. Each day involved making choices and sacrifices in their quest to solve the work-life balance conundrum. Yet achieving true balance in all areas of life is a deeply flawed expectation that can set both women and men up for failure.

The reality for most women is that they aim for some semblance of integration of these elements into their lives, and simply do their best each and every day. Many, upon reflection, recognised that their life happened in stages; there were periods when they focused more on one aspect of their life than others, and as they moved through the different stages their priorities changed.

Own the future

What can we learn from the experiences of others? There are too many traps in making generalisations, and besides, there is not one prescription or process that will guarantee success. Each woman has taken her own path. However, these extraordinary women all shared one common approach — they took control of their future. Their success was based on their ability to take ownership of their careers and take a lead in charting their own future. Despite the obstacles and challenges they faced, they ultimately thrived, and their insights led to the evolution of the success model described below. The THRIVE model outlines the five key ways in which they took responsibility for their career success.

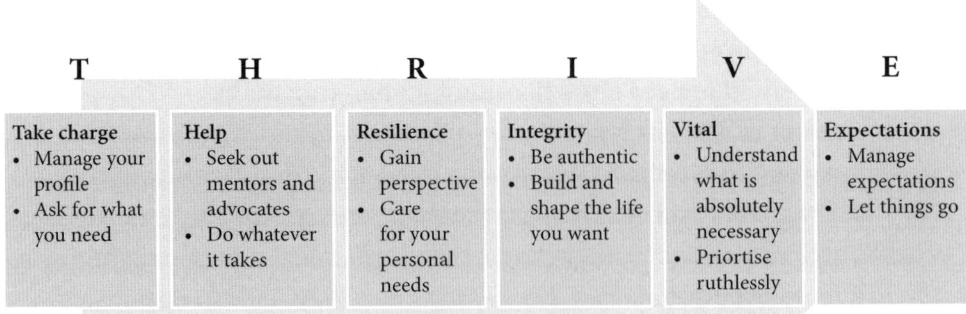

1. Take charge

When you are in the midst of a career interruption, manage your profile. Ensure you keep in touch with work. Out of sight is often out of mind, no matter how invaluable you are. When you are ready to return, set boundaries at home and at work regarding acceptable hours, flexibility and your availability. Learn to say no when arrangements are not going to work for you. Flexible work arrangements will be much easier to negotiate if you are a high performer, so be great at your job. If you need to convince the sceptics, measure your outcomes, seek feedback and demonstrate the success of your new arrangements.

Family-friendly clues abound if you know where to look. When choosing an employer ask yourself some of the following questions: Are there pictures of children and families on senior leaders' desks? When are meetings held — do they start early and finish late or are the times respectful of family needs? Who works flexibly and at what level in the organisation? What are the CEO and senior leaders saying and doing about flexibility?

2. Help

Do whatever it takes. Don't pretend you're fine or you can do it without help. Ensure your partner is a true partner in sharing responsibilities equitably. Involve your family to the extent they and you want. Outsource domestic labour and childcare if that's what you need. Although it may be costly, it may be a wise long-term investment in your career. Ensure you don't neglect important relationships — perhaps plan some quality time with your partner at regular, scheduled intervals.

Mentors and advocates are invaluable. Mentors are often integral to the development of informal networks and gaining access to key decision-makers. They are also a valuable confidential sounding board, someone with whom you can test concerns, feelings or experiences without repercussions. Mentors can also advocate for you when you are absent, allowing you to retain your visibility while you are away.

3. Resilience

Have perspective. You have many chapters in your life. See your situation in the context of your whole life — how does this stage fit in with what you want in life? Your own needs may not be the main game, at least for a while.

Take care of your own needs. Balancing daily chores, childcare, relationships and careers is physically and emotionally exhausting, and we all need downtime. In your quest for caring for others, remember to take care of your own wellbeing. Research shows that prioritising your own needs alongside those of others will minimise chances of burnout and improve your productivity.[2]

4. Integrity

Be authentic. Be the person you want to be, make choices consistent with your values and don't be influenced by the community, society, or others' expectations of how you should live your life. Some women find happiness at home, others in careers, others in both. Recognise that you will be a great role model for your children by being authentic.

Build and shape the life you want. A starting point is to identify what is important in life — in your relationships, family, career and your spiritual needs. Plan it out and then take steps to make it happen. Understand what you are passionate about, what energises you, frustrates you, saps your energy, makes you happy, angry or sad. Let that passion guide you. Pursuing a career that you love, that enables you to bring your best to work and to utilise your key strengths, makes it worthwhile getting out of bed in the morning. Having relationships that are satisfying and empowering provides you with the motivation to keep going. Being spiritually connected may give you a sense of purpose. If, on the other hand, you can't find your passion in your work, ensure you have it in other aspects of your life. Let's face it, we don't all have the dream job, and instead work to live, so we must find ways to incorporate our passions elsewhere in our daily life.

5. Vital

Prioritise ruthlessly. You have no time to waste, so eliminate time-wasters. Efficiency will be paramount, especially when you're back at work. Sheryl Sandberg told Arianna Huffington:

> *'I found that when I cut my office hours dramatically once I had kids, I was not just working less, but I was more productive. Having children forced me to treat every minute of my time as precious.'*[3]

6. Expectations

Let it go. Don't set yourself up for failure by setting unrealistic expectations for yourself. Accept that things won't always be perfect. It may be time to adjust your standards and let go of your quest to be the perfect mother, partner, friend and career woman. Life is a constant trade-off between what you choose to do and what you reject. Don't sweat the small stuff. It's okay if the house is a mess, if punctuality goes out the window, if you get some things wrong. Plan your life, but also recognise that the unexpected happens and setbacks are inevitable. Don't think of them as failures, but as the need to choose another way.

The way forward

'An ounce of practice is worth more than tons of preaching.'
— Mahatma Gandhi

Although *Career Interrupted* focuses on individual stories and experiences, solutions to work-life integration and women's workplace participation must be found beyond the personal experience. Organisations have a serious responsibility to respond to the changing nature of work and life, and create workplaces in which *everyone* can flourish. So find an organisation that can provide for your needs. Workplace culture doesn't have to be a lottery.

The momentum for change is accelerating, with more organisations going beyond producing impressive policy statements to implementing practical action that embeds workplace flexibility and recognises that our work and personal lives can blend successfully. There is the hope that one day we'll look back on this time with bemusement in the same way we're now bemused by the days when women were required to resign employment once they married. Hopefully there will come a time when we'll find it absurd that career breaks were once akin to career suicide.

When that time comes, it will be a sign of lasting change.

Comebacks

People can say shocking or inappropriate things that humiliate us, intentionally or unintentionally, and often we are lost for words. We may slink away or lose our cool, only to think of the perfect retort hours later. These comebacks will help you stay calm and move on from a bad situation. No-one will want to mess with you after you have delivered these lines with confidence and poise!

Question/comment	Comeback	Legal framework
Have you got any children? Do you plan to get pregnant?	Yes, do you?	It is against the law for an employer to ask you if you plan to get pregnant or to ask about your family status and to discriminate against you on the basis of your answer. (Sex Discrimination Act 1984 (Cth), s 7)
How do you know you'll be as good a scientist/lawyer/doctor after you've had the baby?	Did it affect your performance when you became a dad?	
You're pregnant, great. Take the full 12 months off, enjoy your baby and being a mother for as long as you can. Then get back in touch a month or so before you want to return to work and we'll see what we can do.	I'm giving birth to a baby, not losing a brain. Is there any productive work I can get involved in while I'm at home?	
Oh, leaving work early again? Oh, coming in late again?	Yes, I've got a life outside work.	
Are you still working part-time?	Yes. Are you still working full time?	
Are you/when are you planning to start a family?	When do you need to know by?	
Oh, you're pregnant. I think it's about time you finished up.	Is that what happened to you when you became a dad?	
You're pregnant, I guess you won't be getting that promotion then/getting that overseas posting then.	Oh that's right. No-one in the executive team has a family do they?	

Question/comment	Comeback	Legal framework
You're done for, now that you're having a child. Really, you're off our radar now as talent.	Oh that's right. I thought I wanted a career. Turns out I only want the pleasure of working in a mindless job.	It is against the law for an employer to ask you if you plan to get pregnant or to ask about your family status and to discriminate against you on the basis of your answer. (Sex Discrimination Act 1984 (Cth), s 7)
Oh you're pregnant and we just spent $$$ on your development — there's money down the drain!	Really? Well I just might come back. What's the alternative? Don't invest in staff development and end up with dumbos?	
When you come back from maternity leave you'll probably want a behind the scenes job/job with less responsibility, won't you?	Silly me. You're right. I'll never make it as a manager once I've started a family.	
We don't have any women in senior roles, but we only appoint on merit.	You must have a pretty poor talent pool, then.	It is against the law for an employer to discriminate against you on the basis of your sex. (Sex Discrimination Act (Cth), s 5). Perhaps you should analyse your biases and stereotypes.
Our Board is full of men because we can't find women who have the experience.	Is that because your golf club is a men-only club?	Did you know that 80% of men appointed to ASX 200 Company Boards had no previous experience as an ASX 200 Board member either?
You're getting a bit long in the tooth (or any other comment relating to your age).	It's called age, and with it comes experience and wisdom. You might get there too one day.	It is against the law for an employer to ask you about your age and to discriminate against you on the basis of your answer. (Sex Discrimination Act 1984 (Age Discrimination Act 2004 (Cth), s 14)

Question/comment	Comeback	Legal framework
We believe flexible work and part-time arrangements are good for business. We offer it to all our women employees who return to work after having a baby.	That's nice. When will you recognise it as an effective way of doing business and offer it for all roles, rather than as a carrot for good performers?	
You've been porking up lately.	Yeah, I'm going for a world record	Any unwelcome comments of a sexual nature are unlawful including intrusive questions about your appearance (Sex Discrimination Act 1984 (Cth), s 5)
Any kind of sexist comment.	Wow. The 1950s just called. They want your attitude back!	
We don't accommodate part-time or flexible work for anyone here. Everyone has to work standard hours.	You're probably missing out on a huge sector of the workforce then.	Under Victoria's Equal Opportunity Act a prospective employer can't reasonably refuse to accommodate an employee's carer responsibilities. Employers must consider all relevant facts and circumstances and whether the request is reasonable.
Parents judging you at the school gate: 'How can you leave your baby and go to work?'	How can I not? I want to show my girls they can pursue an independent career and don't have to be dependent on a man all their lives.	Latest research by the Harvard Business School shows that children of mothers who pursue careers and fathers who share in the housework are more likely to practice gender equality when they become adults. Working mothers also improve the future prospects of their daughters, who become better educated and earn more.
Teachers at school:'I haven't seen you since the first day of your daughter's school year.'	Yeah that's right. I'm okay with that. How about you?	
Women should be at home with their children.	You know, you're right. A woman's place is in the kitchen. Let me grab a knife.	

Additional Reading

Australian Workforce and Productivity Agency. 2013. *ICT Workforce Study: Meeting Australia's Future ICT Skills Needs.* Australian Government. http://www.industry.gov.au/skills/Publications/Documents/ICT-Workforce-Study-Key-Messages-WEB-2013.pdf.

Barsh, Joanna, and Lareina Yee. *Unlocking The Full Potential Of Women In The US Economy*. McKinsey & Company, 2011.

Bligh, Anna. *Through The Wall: Reflections On Leadership, Love And Survival*. Harper Collins Australia, 2015.

Breekveldt, Norah. *Sideways To The Top: 10 Stories Of Successful Women That Will Change You Thinking About Careers Forever.* Melbourne: Melbourne Books, 2013.

Committee for Economic Development Australia (CEDA). *Women In Leadership: Understanding The Gender Gap*. CEDA, 2013. http://adminpanel.ceda.com.au/folders/Service/Files/Documents/15355~cedawiljune%202013final.pdf.

Ernst & Young Australia. *Untapped Opportunity: The Role Of Women In Unlocking Australia's Productivity Potential*, 2013. http://www.ey.com/Publication/vwLUAssets/Untapped_opportunity_-_The_role_of_women_in_unlocking_Australias_productivity_potential/$FILE/EY-Untapped-opportunity-The-role-of-women-in-unlocking-Australias-productivity-potential.pdf.

Fine, Cordelia. 2010. *Delusions of Gender: The Real Science Behind Sex Discrimination*. New York: Icon Books.

Hewlett, Sylvia Ann. *Off Ramps and On Ramps: Keeping Talented Women on the Road to Success*. Boston, Mass.: Harvard Business School Press, 2007.

Male Champions of Change, Australian Human Rights Commission, *Accelerating the Advancement of Women in Leadership*, 2013.

Rowe, Jessica. *Love. Wisdom. Motherhood.* Crows Nest, NSW: Allen & Unwin, 2011.

Sandberg, Sheryl. 2013. *Lean In: Women Work And The Will To Lead*. Toronto: Knopf Borzoi Books, Random House.

Troiano, Emily V. *Why Diversity Matters*. Catalyst, 2013. http://www.catalyst.org/system/files/why_diversity_matters_catalyst_0.pdf.

Victorian Health Promotion Foundation (VicHealth). 2014. *Findings From The 2013 National Community Attitudes Towards Violence Against Women Survey (NCAS)*. VicHealth.

Workplace Gender Equality Agency. 2012. *Behind The Gender Pay Gap*. Australian Government. https://www.wgea.gov.au/sites/default/files/behind_the_gender_pay_gap_branded.pdf.

Workplace Gender Equality Agency. 2012. *Gender Workplace Statistics At A Glance*. Australian Government.

Workplace Gender Equality Agency. 2013. *Engaging Men In Flexible Work Arrangements*. Australian Government. https://www.wgea.gov.au/sites/default/files/20130829_PP_engaging_men_flex_work_2.pdf.

Notes

Introduction

1 Workplace Gender Equality Agency, 'Gender Workplace Statistics at a Glance', February 2014. Accessed May 2015, https://www.wgea.gov.au/sites/default/files/Stats_at_a_Glance.pdf.
2 ibid.
3 AICD, Company Director, April 2015, p. 6.
4 Workplace Gender Equality Agency, 'Gender Pay Gap Statistics'. Accessed May 2015, https://www.wgea.gov.au/sites/default/files/Gender_Pay_Gap_Factsheet.pdf
5 *The Guardian*, 'Statistics show the gender gap between male and female pay is at 20-year high', 5 September 2014. Accessed 15 July 2015, http://www.theguardian.com/news/datablog/2014/sep/05/statistics-show-the-gender-gap-between-male-and-female-pay-is-at-20-year-high.
6 Workplace Gender Equality Agency, 'Behind the gender pay gap', p. 1. Accessed 15 July 2015, https://www.wgea.gov.au/sites/default/files/behind_the_gender_pay_gap_branded.pdf
7 See research by McKinsey & Co., Catalyst, the Council for Economic Development Australia (CEDA) and the Workplace Gender Equality Agency.
8 Rutherford, S. 2011. Women's Work , Men Cultures, Palgrave Macmillan, Hampshire, UK
9 Sheryl Sandberg and Adam Grant, *New York Times*, 'How Men Can Succeed in the Boardroom and the Bedroom', p. 2. Accessed 15 July 2015, http://nyti.ms/1zOMkGu.
10 Academy of Management, 'The more time fathers spend with their children, the better they fare on the job, new research finds', 8 January 2015. Accessed 15 July 2015, http://aom.org/News/Press-Releases/The-more-time-fathers-spend-with-their-children,-the-better-they-fare-on-the-job,-new-research-finds.aspx.
11 Sandberg and Grant, 'How Men Can Succeed in the Boardroom and the Bedroom', p. 2.
12 ibid, p. 3.
13 Harvard Business School, 'Having a Working Mother is Good for You', 18 May 2015. Accessed 15 July 2015, http://www.hbs.edu/news/releases/Pages/having-a-working-mother.aspx.

14 Workplace Gender Equality Agency, 'Behind the gender pay gap'. Accessed 15 July 2015, https://www.wgea.gov.au/sites/default/files/behind_the_gender_pay_gap_branded.pdf
15 Sandberg and Grant, 'How Men Can Succeed in the Boardroom and the Bedroom', p. 3.

Moira Rayner

1 The Commission was established on January 2014 to minimise and manage misconduct and corruption in the Western Australian public sector and to assist the police in combatting organised crime. The Acting Commissioner takes over the role of the Commissioner when the role is vacant, Commissioner is absent, unable to perform the duties of the Commissioner or unable to act in a certain matter. See: Fergus Shiel, 'The Price Of Friendship', *The Age*, 2005. Accessed 6 July 2015, http://www.theage.com.au/news/general/the-price-of-friendship/2005/10/28/1130400361078.htm.
2 ibid.
3 ibid.
4 Daniel Goleman, *Emotional Intelligence* (London: Bloomsbury, 1996).
5 The Spiritual Exercises are a compilation of meditations, prayers and contemplative practices developed by St Ignatius Loyola to help people deepen their relationship with God. See: *Ignatian Spirituality*, 2015, 'The Spiritual Exercises – Ignatianspirituality.Com'. Accessed 6 July 2015, http://www.ignatianspirituality.com/ignatian-prayer/the-spiritual-exercises.
6 See: Daniel J Siegel, *Mindsight* (Carlton North, Vic.: Scribe Publications, 2009); Norman Doidge, *The Brain That Changes Itself* (Carlton North, Vic.: Scribe Publications, 2007); Jeffrey Schwartz and Sharon Begley, *The Mind And The Brain* (New York: Regan Books/HarperCollins Publ., 2003).
7 Joan Kirner and Moira Rayner, *The Women's Power Handbook* (Ringwood, Vic.: Viking, 1999), pp. 39–47.

Her Excellency Frances Adamson

1 Catalyst, *The Double-Bind Dilemma For Women In Leadership: Damned If You Do, Doomed If You Don't* (Catalyst, 2007), http://www.catalyst.org/knowledge/double-bind-dilemma-women-leadership-damned-if-you-do-doomed-if-you-dont-0.

Dr Margeurite Evans-Galea

1 Committee on Maximizing the Potential of Women in Academic Science and Engineering (National Academies), *Beyond Bias And Barriers: Fulfilling The Potential Of Women In Academic Science And Engineering* (Washington: The National Academies Press, 2007), p. 5.

2 Catherine Fox, *7 Myths About Women And Work* (Sydney: NewSouth Publishing, 2012).

3 Organisation for Economic Cooperation and Development: An international organisation comprising 34 member states whose mission 'is to promote policies that will improve the economic and social well-being of people around the world'. See: OECD.org, 2015. 'About The OECD'. Accessed 7 July 2015. http://www.oecd.org/about/.

4 Engineers Australia, *Women In Engineering: A Statistical Update* (Engineers Australia, 2012), p. 2, https://www.engineersaustralia.org.au/sites/default/files/shado/Representation/Information_Papers/women_in_engineering_2012.pdf.

5 ibid, p. 3.

6 ibid, p. 4.

7 ibid, p. 18.

8 Melanie Sanders et al., *Creating a Positive Cycle: Critical Steps to Achieving Gender Parity in Australia* (Bain & Company Australia, 2013), http://www.bain.com/offices/australia/en_us/publications/creating-a-positive-cycle.aspx.

9 Committee on Maximizing the Potential of Women in Academic Science and Engineering (National Academies), *Beyond Bias*, p. 5.

10 Professor Simon Marginson FASSA et al., *Country Comparisons: International Comparisons of Science, Technology, Engineering and Mathematics (STEM) Education* (Australian Council of Learned Academies, 2013), p. 13, p. 16. http://www.acola.org.au/PDF/SAF02Consultants/SAF02_STEM_%20FINAL.pdf.

11 Emily V. Troiano, *Why Diversity Matters*, Catalyst, 2013. http://www.catalyst.org/system/files/why_diversity_matters_catalyst_0.pdf

12 Norah Breekveldt, *Sideways To The Top: 10 Stories Of Successful Women That Will Change Your Thinking About Careers Forever* (Melbourne: Melbourne Books, 2013), pp. 15–17.

13 Justin Harmon, 'Blind Orchestra Auditions Better For Women, Study Finds', *News At Princeton*, 2000, http://www.princeton.edu/main/news/archive/A94/90/73G00/.

14 Joanna Barsh and Lareina Yee, *Unlocking The Full Potential Of Women In The US Economy* (McKinsey & Company, 2011), http://www.mckinsey.com/client_service/organization/latest_thinking/unlocking_the_full_potential.

15 Sheryl Sandberg, *Lean In* (London: WH Allen, 2013).

16 Ernst & Young Australia, *Untapped Opportunity: The Role Of Women In Unlocking Australia's Productivity Potential*, 2013. http://www.ey.com/Publication/vwLUAssets/Untapped_opportunity_-_The_role_of_women_in_unlocking_Australias_productivity_potential/$FILE/EY-Untapped-opportunity-The-role-of-women-in-unlocking-Australias-productivity-potential.pdf.

17 Friedreich's ataxia is a rare inherited disease that causes nervous system damage and movement problems that usually begins in childhood and leads to impaired muscle coordination and an early death.
18 Breekveldt, *Sideways To The Top*, p. 276.
19 ibid, p. 226.

Anna Burke and Kelly O'Dwyer

1 They include Jackie Kelly, Michelle O'Byrne, Tanya Plibersek, Natasha Stott Despoja, Nicola Roxon, Kirsten Livermore, Sophie Mirabella and Catherine King. See: Dr Mark Rodrigues, *Children In The Parliamentary Chambers* (Department of Parliamentary Services, 2009).
2 For a more complete discussion of these issues, see the full transcript of Kelly O'Dwyer's speech in the Federal Parliament on 26 February 2015, entitled 'Matter of Public Importance: The Importance of Childcare'. See: Kellyodwyer.com.au, 2015, 'Matter Of Public Importance – The Importance Of Childcare | Kelly O'dwyer'. Accessed 8 July 2015, http://www.kellyodwyer.com.au/matter-of-public-importance-the-importance-of-childcare/.
3 Parliament of Australia, *House of Representatives Procedure Report: Chapter 5 Current and Emerging Issues* (Standing Committee on Procedure, 2011).
4 aph.gov.au, 2015. 'Appendix 1: Women In National Parliaments – Top 50 Ranked Countries 2013 With 2008 And 2001 Compared – Parliament Of Australia '. Accessed July 8 2015. http://www.aph.gov.au/About_Parliament/Parliamentary_Departments/Parliamentary_Library/pubs/rp/rp1415/WomanAustParl/Append1.
5 Norman Abjorensen, 'Political Rivalry: What's New?', *The Drum (ABC News)*, 2011, http://www.abc.net.au/news/2011-12-09/abjorensen-political-rivalry-what-new/3722680.
6 webcity.com.au, 2015, 'Paul Keating Insults'. Accessed 8 July 2015, http://www.webcity.com.au/keating/.
7 YouTube, 2015. 'Julia Gillard's Misogyny Speech'. Accessed 8 July 2015, https://www.youtube.com/watch?v=SOPsxpMzYw4.
8 Anna Bligh, *Through The Wall* (Harper Collins Australia, 2015).

Lucinda Nolan

1 Colleen A. Woolley and Janet S. Eury, *Arresting Women* (Brunswick, Vic.: Victoria Press, 1997); 'Women in Policing Exhibit', in *International Association Of Women Police 10th Annual Conference*, 1972.
2 Christine Nixon and Jo Chandler, *Fair Cop* (Carlton, Vic.: Victory Books, 2012).
3 Christine Nixon and Jo Chandler, *Fair Cop* (Carlton, Vic.: Victory Books, 2012), Ch. 3.

Lisa Croxford

1 Victorian Equal Opportunity and Human Rights Commission, *Changing The Rules: The Experiences Of Female Lawyers In Victoria* (Carlton, Vic.: Victorian Equal Opportunity and Human Rights Commission, 2012), p. 39.
2 Lisa Croxford, *Employment Insight: Bystander Actions – The Next Frontier For Managing Behaviour At Work*, Legal Briefings (Herbert Smith Freehills, 2013), http://www.herbertsmithfreehills.com/insights/legal-briefings/bystander-actions-the-next-frontier-for-managing-behaviour-at-work.
3 Norah Breekveldt, *Sideways To The Top: 10 Stories Of Successful Women That Will Change Your Thinking About Careers Forever* (Melbourne: Melbourne Books, 2013), pp. 15–17.

Tracey Spicer

1 Women in the Media Team, 'Where Are The Women In The Media?', *New Matilda*, 2013, https://newmatilda.com/2013/03/08/where-are-women-media.
2 Australian Bureau of Statistics, *Australia's Birth Rate Falls, But Older Mothers Buck The Trend*, 2014, http://www.abs.gov.au/ausstats/abs@.nsf/latestProducts/3301.0Media%20Release12013.
3 Tracy Spicer, 'Dear Mr Sexist', *The Hoopla*, 2012, http://thehoopla.com.au/dear-misogynist/.
4 Tracey Spicer, 'This Is What I Look Like Without Make-Up', Blog, *Tracey's Writings Thoughts, Words, Actions*, 2014,

Lucinda Dunn, OAM

1 Emma Sandall, 'Interview With Maina Gielgud', emmasandell.com, Accessed 9 July 2015, http://emmasandall.com/interview-with-maina-gielgud-ao/.
2 Kitty Walker, 'Waiting For Baby: What Our Dancers Do While They're Pregnant', *Behind Ballet*, 5 August 2011, Accessed 9 July 2015, http://www.behindballet.com/waiting-for-baby-what-our-dancers-do-while-theyre-pregnant/.

Lucy Roland

1 Names of the business and manager have been changed.
2 D&B Small Business, *Women Entrepreneurs Double but Barriers Remain*, News. Accessed 9 July 2015, http://dnbsmallbusiness.com.au/News/Women_entrepreneurs_double_but_barriers_remain/indexdl_9774.aspx.

3 Australian Women Chamber of Commerce & Industry, *National Research On Women Business Owners & Female Entrepreneurs* (Australian Women Chamber of Commerce & Industry), p. 39. Accessed 9 July 2015, http://www.security4women.org.au/wp-content/uploads/AWCCI_National-Research-RegionalvsMetro_12.pdf.

4 Sabrina Parsons, 'Women Are Stronger Than Men – In Entrepreneurship', *Forbes*, 5 March 2011. Accessed 9 July 2015, http://www.forbes.com/sites/sabrinaparsons/2011/05/03/women-are-stronger-than-men-in-entrepreneurship/.

5 Australian Bureau of Statistics, *4102.0 – Australian Social Trends, Sep 2012: Education Differences Between Men And Women* (Canberra: Australian Bureau of Statistics, 2012).

6 The Australian Institute of Health and Welfare, *Australia's Mothers And Babies 2009* (Canberra: Australian Government, 2011).

7 According to the ABS in 2006, women employed full-time spent six hours and 39 minutes per day taking care of dependent children, up 49 minutes over the past nine years. This is compared to men in full-time employment, who spent three hours and 43 minutes per day taking care of their children, unchanged over the same time period. See: D&B Small Business, *Women Entrepreneurs Double but Barriers Remain*, News. Accessed 9 July 2015, http://dnbsmallbusiness.com.au/News/Women_entrepreneurs_double_but_barriers_remain/indexdl_9774.aspx.

8 Ernst & Young Australia, *Untapped Opportunity: The Role Of Women In Unlocking Australia's Productivity Potential*, 2013. http://www.ey.com/Publication/vwLUAssets/Untapped_opportunity_-_The_role_of_women_in_unlocking_Australias_productivity_potential/$FILE/EY-Untapped-opportunity-The-role-of-women-in-unlocking-Australias-productivity-potential.pdf.

9 Clare O'Neil, 'More Women In Work Key To Productivity', *The Australian*, 10 March 2014. Accessed 10 July 2015, http://www.theaustralian.com.au/national-affairs/opinion/more-women-in-work-key-to-productivity/story-e6frgd0x-1226849604391.

10 Arianna Huffington, *Thrive: He Third Metric To Redefining Success And Creating A Life Of Well-Being, Wisdom, And Wonder* (Harmony, 2014), p. 68.

Dr Sharon Lierse

1 Geert H. Hofstede, *Culture's Consequences: Comparing Values, Behaviors, Institutions, and Organizations Across Nations*, 2nd ed. (Thousand Oaks, Calif.: Sage Publications, 2001).

2 Geert-hofstede.com, 2015. 'Malaysia – Geert Hofstede'. Accessed 10 July 2015, http://geert-hofstede.com/malaysia.html; Geert-hofstede.com, 2015, 'Australia – Geert Hofstede'. Accessed 10 July 2015, http://geert-hofstede.com/australia.html.

3 ibid.

Dr Hannah Piterman

1 Christina Fox, 'The Hidden Problem Of Domestic Violence', *Christianity Today*, March 2015, http://www.todayschristianwoman.com/articles/2015/march/hidden-problem-of-domestic-violence.html.
2 Australian Domestic and Family Violence Clearinghouse (ADFVC), *Domestic Violence And The Workplace Employee: Employer And Union Resources*, 2011, http://www.adfvc.unsw.edu.au/PDF%20files/Domestic_Violence_Workplace_resource.pdf.
3 Names have been changed.
4 Victorian Health Promotion Foundation (VicHealth), *Australians' Attitudes To Violence Against Women: Findings From The 2013 National Community Attitudes Towards Violence Against Women Survey (NCAS 2013)* (VicHealth, 2015).
5 Hannah Piterman et al., 'Domestic Violence: It is Time for the Medical Profession to Play its Part', *Internal Medicine Journal*, vol. 45, no. 5, May 2015, pp. 471–596, p. 471.
6 Domestic Violence Victoria, dvvic.org.au.
7 ibid.
8 abc.net.au, 'Thirty-One Women Killed In Australia In 15 Weeks Renews Call For Action'. Accessed 13 July 2015, http://www.abc.net.au/7.30/content/2015/s4215739.htm.
9 David Cassar, 'Understanding Family Violence: Key Statistics', dvvic.org.au. Accessed 13 July 2015, http://www.dvvic.org.au/index.php/understanding-family-violence/key-statistics.html.
10 Victorian Health Promotion Foundation (VicHealth), *Australians' Attitudes To Violence Against Women: Findings From The 2013 National Community Attitudes Towards Violence Against Women Survey – Research Summary (NCAS)* (VicHealth, 2014).
11 Department of Parliamentary Services, *Domestic Violence in Australia: An Overview of the Issues*, Liesl Mitchell, 23 November 2011.
12 Anna Whitelaw, 'Deer Park woman found dead in suspected murder-suicide', *The Age*, 15 December 2014. Accessed 13 July 2015, http://www.theage.com.au/victoria/deer-park-woman-found-dead-in-suspected-murdersuicide-20141214-126qy2.html#ixzz3fjgDSU8v.
13 See: Name Withheld, 'This Man is Violent and He is Nearby', *The Age*, 15 December 2014. Accessed 13 July 2015, http://www.theage.com.au/comment/the-age-letters/this-man-is-violent-and-he-is-nearby-20141215-127lqm.html#ixzz3fji3x7o1; Tim Cartwright, 'Remembering Masa Vukotic on our journey of understanding', *The Age*, 23 March 2015. Accessed 13 July 2015, http://www.theage.com.au/comment/remembering-masa-vukotic-on-our-journey-of-understanding-20150323-1m5b3c.html#ixzz3fjkTUB2v.

14 New South Wales Bureau of Crime Statistics and Research, 'Reporting Violence to Police: A survey of victims attending domestic violence services', Emma Birdsey and Lucy Snowball, 2013.
15 Diana Rose et al., 'Barriers and Facilitators of Disclosures of Domestic Violence by Mental Health Service Users: Qualitative Study', *The British Journal of Psychiatry*, vol. 8, no. 3, February 2011, pp. 189–194.
16 VicHealth, NCAS – Research Summary.
17 Crime and Misconduct Commission Queensland (CMC), 'Policing Domestic Violence in Queensland: Meeting the Challenges' (Brisbane, CMC, 2005).
18 ADFVC, 'Better Policing, Better Outcomes: Changing police culture to prevent domestic violence and homicide', Gaby Marcus (Sydney, ADFVC, 2009).
19 Department of Human Services, 'Family And Domestic Violence', humanservices.gov.au. Accessed 13 July 2015, http://www.humanservices.gov.au/customer/subjects/domestic-and-family-violence.
20 Australian Law Reform Commission (ALRC), 'Family Violence and Commonwealth Laws: Improving Legal Frameworks' (Sydney, ALRC, 2011), http://www.alrc.gov.au/sites/default/files/pdfs/publications/whole_alrc_117.pdf.
21 VicHealth, 'Preventing Violence Before it Occurs: A Framework and Background Paper to Guide the Primary Prevention of Violence Against Women in Victoria' (Carlton South, VicHealth, 2007), http://www.dvvic.org.au/attachments/2007_vichealth_pvaw.framework.pdf.
22 Australian Human Rights Commission (AHRC), 'Encourage. Support. Act! Bystander Approaches to Sexual Harassment in the Workplace', Paula McDonald and Michael Flood (AHRC, 2012), https://www.humanrights.gov.au/sites/default/files/content/sexualharassment/bystander/bystander_june2012.pdf.
23 Women's Health Victoria, 'Take A Stand Against Domestic Violence', *whv.org.au*. Accessed 13 July 2015, http://whv.org.au/what-we-do/take-a-stand-against-domestic-violence.
24 VicHealth and Australian Football League, 'Building Cultures of Respect and Non-Violence: A Review of Literature Concerning Adult Learning and Violence Prevention Programs with Men', Sue Dyson and Michael Flood, 2008.
25 ABC News, 'Anti-domestic violence campaigner Rosie Batty says the process for reporting abuse "has to change" to help victims break their silence"', *ABC News*, 24 February 2015. Accessed 13 July 2015, http://www.abc.net.au/news/2015-02-24/anti-domestic-violence-campaigner-rosie-batty-reporting-change/6232718.
26 Marilyn French, 'The War Against Women' (London, Penguin, 1992).

Dr Jennifer Whelan

1 Maitland and P. Thomson, *Future Work: Changing Organizational Culture For The New World of Work*, (Palgrave Macmillan, 2014).
2 Australian Bureau of Statistics, 2006.
3 Catalyst, 'The Great Debate: Flexibility Vs. Face Time – Busting Myths Behind Flexible Work Arrangements', 2013.
4 Australian Human Rights Commission & Male Champions of Change. 'Accelerating the Advancement of Women in Leadership', 2012.
5 J. Whelan, 'Barriers to Equality of Opportunity in the Workforce'. *Women in Leadership: Understanding the Gender Gap*. Committee for Economic Development of Australia, 2013.
6 J. C. Williams, M. Blair-Loy, and J. L. Berdahl, 'Cultural Schema, social class and flexibility schema'. *Journal of Social Issues*, Vol. 69 (2), 2013, pp. 209–234.
7 J. Lynch, 'Work-life balance? Take condoms, says Southern Cross Austereo radio boss', *Sydney Morning Herald*, March 2015.
8 Australian Institute of Management, 'Managing in a Flexible Work Environment', 2013.
9 J. Heerwagen, J. Kelly and K. Kampschroer, 'The Changing Nature of Organizations, Work and Workplace', National Institute of Building Sciences, US, 2010.
10 Maitland and P. Thomson, *Future Work*, 2014.
11 Senate Estimates, 2013.
12 The 100% Project, 'Men at Work: What They Want and How Unconscious Bias Stops Them Getting It', 2012.
13 Catalyst, 'The Great Debate'.

Samone McCurdy

1 Michael E Lamb, *The Role Of The Father In Child Development* (Hoboken, N.J, Wiley, 2004).
2 Diversity Council Australia, 'Men Get Flexible! Mainstreaming Flexible Work in Australian Business' by Graeme Russell and Jane O'Leary, (Sydney, 2012); Gillian Whitehouse et al., 'The Parental Leave in Australia Survey: November 2006 Report', (2006).
3 AHRC, 'Supporting Working Parents: Pregnancy and Return to Work National Review', (Sydney, AHRC, 2014), accessed June 2, 2015, https://www.humanrights.gov.au/sites/default/files/document/publication/SWP_Report_2014.pdf
4 Father Involvement Research Alliance, 'The Effects of Father Involvement: An Updated Research Summary of the Evidence', by Sarah Allen and Kerry Daly, (Guelph, Centre for Families Work & Well-Being, 2007), http://www.fira.ca/cms/documents/29/Effects_of_Father_Involvement.pdf

5 Samone McCurdy, 'The Coalition's Paid Parental Leave Scheme: What Are We Really Signing Up For?' *Communities, Children and Families Australia*, vol. 8, no. 2, p. 5-12.
6 Maria C. Huerta et al., 'Fathers' Leave, Fathers' Involvement and Child Development: Are they Related Evidence from Four OECD Countries?' (Paris, Organization for Economic Co-operation and Development, 2013), http://www.oecd.org/officialdocuments/publicdisplaydocumentpdf/?cote=DELSA/ELSA/WD/SEM(2012)11&docLanguage=En
7 Ray Broomhill and Rhonda Sharp, 'Australia's Parental Leave Policy and Gender Equality: An International Comparison', (Adelaide, Australian Workplace Innovation and Social Research Centre, 2012), http://www.adelaide.edu.au/wiser/pubs/WISeR_Parental_Leave_Policy_and_Gender_Equality_an_international_comparison_report.pdf
8 Linda Haas and Tine Rostgaard, 'Fathers' Rights to Paid Parental Leave in the Nordic Countries: Consequences for the Gendered Division of Leave', *Community Work and Family*, vol. 14, no. 2, May 2011.
9 Department of Families, Housing, Community Services and Indigenous Affairs (DFHCSIA), 'Paid Parental Leave Evaluation: Phase 1', by Bill Martin et al., (Canberra, DFHCSIA, 2012), https://www.dss.gov.au/sites/default/files/documents/06_2012/op44.pdf; Centre for Work and Life (CWL), 'Australian Work and Life Index: Living, Working and Caring in Australia' by Natalie Skinner and Barbara Pocock, (Adelaide, CWL, 2014), http://www.unisa.edu.au/documents/eass/cwl/publications/awali_2014_national_report_final.pdf

Conclusions

1 Thanks to Samone McCurdy for contributing to these reflections.
2 Sheryl Sandberg and Adam Grant, 'Madam C.E.O., Get Me a Coffee: Women Doing "Office Housework"', 6 February 2015. Accessed 15 July 2015, http://www.nytimes.com/2015/02/08/opinion/sunday/sheryl-sandberg-and-adam-grant-on-women-doing-office-housework.html.
3 Arianna Huffington, *Thrive: He Third Metric To Redefining Success And Creating A Life Of Well-Being, Wisdom, And Wonder* (Harmony, 2014), p. 68.

Acknowledgements

It gives me great pleasure to acknowledge the extensive help I have received from family, friends and colleagues.

My greatest debt is to my husband, Andrew Katona, whose unconditional support, encouragement and love urged me on through the highs and lows of writing this book.

This book would not have been possible without the generosity of spirit of the women profiled herein, and their courage in sharing their life experiences and reflections, some of them deeply personal.

I am deeply grateful to the many colleagues and friends who have opened doors for me to meet the amazing women profiled here, and whose insights, perspectives and wise judgment were immensely valuable in helping me shape this book. In particular, I thank Kate Jenkins, Commissioner for the Victorian Equal Opportunity and Human Rights Commission, for her generosity in opening her networks to me, to lend weight to this book and to support its entry into the publishing world. I also want to acknowledge Sarah Rey and Mary-Jane Ierodiaconou, founders of Justitia Lawyers, who encouraged, supported and advocated for me at every step, and represent the greatest examples I know of women who enable other women to achieve their best.

Finally, I would like to thank the terrific team at Melbourne Books, especially David Tenenbaum, Chloe Brien and Anya Trybala, whose exceptional editorial talents helped sharpen the drafts into a compelling book and who quelled my anxieties at critical times.